Foreword

When it released the Macintosh in 1984, Apple invented what we now know as the personal computer.

It's been a long time since then. The internet came. Mobile phone and data networks. Google and Facebook. Our world is a different place now, and we expect different things of the technology we buy.

Yet amid this new age of smartphones and tablets (invented in their present form, once again, by Apple), one personal computer brand is thriving and growing.

Every year, more and more people discover what makes Macs different. We've been writing about it since the start, and we still can't easily describe it.

We're not paid by Apple. We just like the things they make. And we hope this guide helps you enjoy them.

Adam Banks
Editor in Chief
MacUser
@macusermagazine

Contents

iCloud makes it all work together p104

1 Hardware

The Apple range p8

MacBook Pro with Retina display p10
MacBook Air p16
MacBook Pro p19

Apple add-ons
Apple TV, AirPort, Thunderbolt Display,
USB SuperDrive, Apple Keyboards p22

2 OS X

The Mac desktop
The Dock p28
The Mac menu bar p30

Running apps
Switching between apps p33
Mission Control p34
Dashboard Widgets p35

Spotlight
Searching your Mac p36

Accessibility
Seeing and hearing controls,
VoiceOver, Dictation p38

User accounts
Setting up and switching p40
Parental Controls p41

Backing up your files
Time Machine p42
Versions p43

Networking your Mac
Choosing a router; wifi setup p44
Sharing files p45
Sharing with PCs p46

Windows on the Mac

Compatibility p66
How to buy Windows p67
32 or 64-bit? p68
Installing with Boot Camp p69
Security in Windows p71
Running Windows apps free p71
Parallels and VMware Fusion p72

4

3 Apps

Installing apps
The Mac App Store p78
Gatekeeper p78

Preview and TextEdit
Understanding Versions p80
Signing forms p82
Plain text vs rich text p83

iMovie and GarageBand p84
iPhoto p86

iWork
Pages p92
Numbers p94
Keynote p94

Microsoft Office
Word, Excel, PowerPoint and Outlook p95

Apple's Pro apps p96
Adobe Creative Cloud p98
Games on the Mac p100

4 iCloud

iCloud and iOS devices
Managing your storage p105
Contacts, Calendars and Notes p106
iCloud Tabs p107

Documents in the Cloud p108
Dropbox p109

Photo Stream p110

Connecting on the go
Setting up a service order p47
Tethering and connection sharing p48

Sharing and messaging
Centralised accounts; social networks p50
Messages and FaceTime p51

Mail p52
Reminders, Calendar and Notifications . . . p54
Safari p56

iTunesp
Managing your library p58
iTunes' new look explained p59

Image Capture p62
Energy Saver p64
Windows on the Mac p66

5 Accessories

**The best stands, cases, drives
and batteries for your MacBook** p116

6 Maintenance

Watching for trouble
Checking disk usage and making room p123
Disk Utility p124
When apps crash p125
Keychain p126
Using the Terminal p126
When the worst happens p127

Gestures explained p128
Glossary p130

Chapter 1
Hardware

The Apple range

*Apple computers and devices come in all shapes and sizes.
Here's how the MacBooks fit into the current line-up.*

MacBook Pro Retina

More pixels, in the world's sleekest computer case.

MacBook Pro

The laptop that set the standard.

MacBook Air

Incredibly thin, yet with nothing taken out.

iPod touch
The world's leading game console.

iPad Retina
Latest full-size tablet.

iPad mini
Small but mighty.

iPhone
The most mobile.

Mac mini
An affordable desktop Mac.
Bring your own monitor.

Mac Pro
Serious power, serious cash.

iMac
The mainstream Mac.

MacBook Pro with Retina display

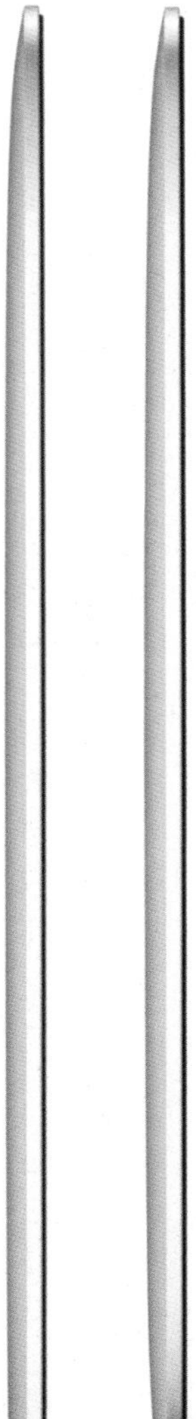

Apple's ultimate laptop

As radical as they are, Apple's Retina machines are still recognisable as MacBooks, with their familiar finish, curves and details. The Unibody shell, carved from a single piece of aluminium, is a technical masterpiece, and with the thickness of the whole case substantially shaved, the blade-like elegance of the design is even more striking.

There are many imitators, but no laptop on the market can match the uncompromising engineering prowess that the MacBook Pro with Retina display exudes. Given ten times the budget, you couldn't buy a more beautiful computer, or shoehorn more capable components into the sliver of space within it.

The Retina display concept, introduced with the iPhone 4 and followed in the third-generation iPad, was coined by Apple to describe a screen whose resolution is so high that, in use, it's impossible to make out the individual pixels with the naked eye. The liquid crystal dots that make up the screen are so small and

→ Seen here at actual size, the 13in Retina MacBook Pro is a marvel of industrial design, tesselating more into the Unibody than should fit.

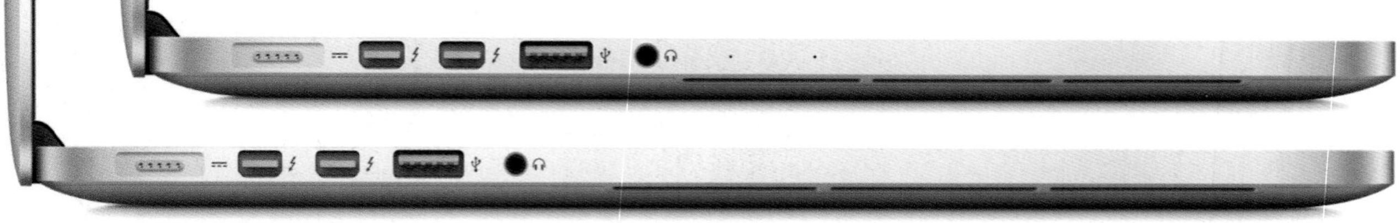

tightly packed that human vision can't resolve them; the picture is, to all intents and purposes, as continuous and seamless as our retinal image of the real world.

There are debates about exactly how this claim should be judged, but neither objective nor subjective measures find these machines wanting. In launching the 15in Retina model, the first to appear, Apple retained the same panel size (15.4 inches along the diagonal, to be exact) as the MacBook Pro and doubled the number of pixels per linear inch, giving four times the resolution. At 2880 × 1800, the screen has more than five megapixels. Inevitably, it looks startlingly sharp.

Quality and precision aside, a simple benefit is that video editors can play every pixel of Full HD, as seen on 50in flat-screen TVs, or indeed the 2K format widely used in digital cinemas, *and still have more than half the screen to spare.*

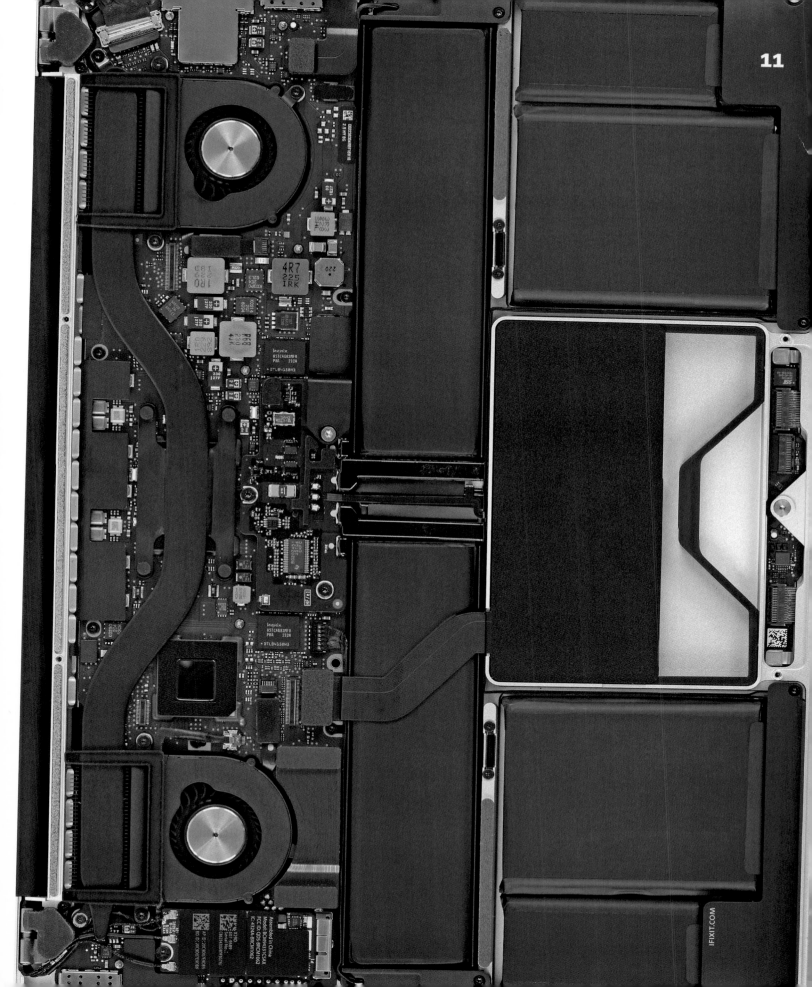

↓ The Retina MacBook Pro manages to make the regular model look chunky. There's no room at all for internal expansion (even the RAM is sealed), but with two Thunderbolt and two USB 3 ports, external add-ons can be super-fast.

This monster resolution demands a serious dedicated graphics chipset, and somehow Apple has crammed in a highly capable NVIDIA GPU, the GeForce GT 650M with 1GB of GDDR5 memory. Remarkably, if the enormous native screen resolution still doesn't satisfy your requirements, the NVIDIA can simultaneously drive two additional external displays with a resolution of up to 2560 × 1600 pixels each.

The 13in Retina model adopts exactly that resolution for its built-in LCD, making it equivalent to a 27in iMac (in fact, it has more space than the desktop machine, thanks to its slightly taller aspect ratio). This reduced pixel count compared to the 15in helps it to get away with only Intel's modest HD Graphics 4000 chip (the 15in's fall-back GPU), which we'd expect to be upgraded at the earliest opportunity, now that even the little MacBook Air has the more powerful new HD Graphics 5000.

This compromise does make the price of the 13in more approachable, while the 15in is the obvious choice for graphics and video professionals, who'll enjoy blazing performance.

Running creative software

Apps such as Final Cut Pro, Adobe After Effects and Maya are obvious candidates, but buyers must look at whether their apps have been updated for Retina, because it's not easy to make sense of the high-density screen without specially written software. Adobe has made progress with its update programme, significantly bringing InDesign, its desktop publishing app, up to Retina spec and finally making page layout on a laptop look credible after all these years.

Both Retina sizes have that slightly-squarer-than-TV 16:10 widescreen aspect ratio, and both nominally come with a gloss finish – but in fact this is a little less glossy than previous MacBooks, for an interesting reason. In designing a much thinner laptop, Apple had to look for

MacBook Pro with Retina display

13-inch 2.5GHz with Retina display

2.5GHz dual-core Intel Core i5
Turbo Boost up to 3.1GHz
8GB 1600MHz RAM
128GB SSD
Intel HD Graphics 4000
2560 × 1600 display
7 hour battery

13-inch 2.5GHz with Retina display

2.6GHz dual-core Intel Core i5
Turbo Boost up to 3.2GHz
8GB 1600MHz RAM
256GB SSD
Intel HD Graphics 4000
2560 × 1600 display
7 hour battery

15-inch 2.4GHz with Retina display

2.4GHz quad-core Intel Core i7
Turbo Boost up to 3.4GHz
8GB 1600MHz RAM
256GB SSD
Intel HD Graphics 4000
NVIDIA GeForce GT 650M
with 1GB of GDDR5 memory
2880 × 1800 display
7 hour battery

15-inch 2.7GHz with Retina display

2.7GHz quad-core Intel Core i7
Turbo Boost up to 3.7GHz
16GB 1600MHz RAM
512GB SSD
Intel HD Graphics 4000
NVIDIA GeForce GT 650M
with 1GB of GDDR5 memory
2880 × 1800 display
7 hour battery

depth and weight wins everywhere, and settled on a new manufacturing process for the screen that integrates the front glass – the part you can actually touch – with the LCD panel itself.

So there's no glass protecting the display; the front *is* glass, but so thin it bends like plastic if you press it hard, and if you did happen to scratch it you'd have to replace the entire assembly – likely to be by far the most expensive component. It does look fantastic, although still a little too shiny for those who order their MacBook Pros with the matt screen.

Please do not touch Where there *is* still glass is on the trackpad, which as always is supremely usable. It's understandable that Apple doesn't see the need for a touchscreen on its laptops when this system feels so right – and who wants fingerprints all over what they're trying to look at anyway? Gestures play an increasing role in OS X, making it easier to control everyday features without stopping to think. We've summarised the most common gestures on p128.

Somehow, keyboard backlighting has still been squeezed in, and it does help in dark studios, meetings, conferences and wherever light is low. Its intensity can be adjusted from the keyboard itself, so you can quickly kill the glare when ambient lighting dims and leaves you glowing like plutonium. The backlight can also be turned off to conserve battery life – al-

though at a typical seven hours, that's not necessarily a pressing concern. Apple's quoted figures are always realistic, too, so you should be able to work through an intercontinental flight without worries.

All Retina models come with at least 8GB RAM as standard, which is just as well because it's impossible to upgrade later. The highest standard configuration has 16, and creative pros should think about paying the extra for that in other configurations as future-proofing, although 8GB with SSD storage will feel extremely responsive in almost any task.

And all Retina models are indeed equipped with solid state drives, since a clunky mechanical hard disk would be a fish out of water here. With SSDs still coming at high cost prices, though, the entry-level 13in Retina has only half the storage of the cheapest MacBook Pro.

While the options for internal upgrades are limited, you do get a choice of CPUs, SSD sizes and so on when you order from the online Apple Store, and the inclusion of Thunderbolt as well as USB 3 opens up excellent prospects for external expansion. Just choose carefully between the highly portable, relatively affordable 13in and the no-holds-barred 15in when you put your money down.

The classic

The MacBook Pro hasn't changed dramatically in many years – and you can see why not. Its Unibody shell exudes quality, and inside are all the bits you could wish for, including an 8x SuperDrive, which reads and writes all DVD formats (Apple doesn't support Blu-ray). It's the only Mac left that has such a drive, following the effective demise of the old Mac Pro.

But the MacBook Pro hasn't slipped behind the times. Every model is regularly updated, with faster parts like the new multi-core Core i5 and Core i7 processors keeping performance up with the best laptops around. Apple was the first computer maker to introduce Thunderbolt ports, and every MacBook Pro now has one as standard, alongside two USB 3 ports, FireWire 800 (phased out on other Macs) and Gigabit Ethernet. Although having only one Thunderbolt port is slightly limiting, you can daisychain up to seven devices from it, including two monitors, as long as all but one of them have a second pass-through port. Between Thunderbolt, FireWire 800 and USB 3, you should have no trouble finding fast storage and other essential peripherals.

Every MacBook Pro has an integrated Intel HD Graphics chip that's capable of running its built-in screen and an external display up to 2560 × 1600 at the same time. In the 15in, this is complemented by a choice of dedicated NVIDIA GPUs with their own video memory, which kick in when more demanding graphics processing is required.

Apple no longer sells the 17in model that used to be popular with creative professionals. It was discontinued at the same time the Retina models appeared, and in some ways they serve the same purpose. Another option for graphics users remains available: while every MacBook comes with a mirror-like glossy screen as standard, the 15in MacBook is also available with a matt anti-glare finish. This changes the appearance of the machine, too, because the black surround, which sits under the front glass, is replaced by a silver-coloured bezel. The anti-glare screen has a higher resolution than the standard 15in panel,

POINTS OF NOTE

- ☐ **Only MacBook with a SuperDrive**
- ☐ **Lots of build-to-order options on 15in**
- ☐ **Big hard disk capacities**
- ☐ **Only one Thunderbolt port**
- ☐ **RAM and hard disk are upgradable**

MacBook Pro

13-inch 2.5GHz

2.5GHz dual-core Intel Core i5
Turbo Boost up to 3.1GHz
4GB 1600MHz RAM
500GB 5400rpm hard drive
Intel HD Graphics 4000
1280 × 800 display
7 hour battery

13-inch 2.9GHz

2.9GHz dual-core Intel Core i7
Turbo Boost up to 3.6GHz
8GB 1600MHz RAM
750GB 5400rpm hard drive
Intel HD Graphics 4000
1280 × 800 display
7 hour battery

15-inch 2.3GHz

2.3GHz quad-core Intel Core i7
Turbo Boost up to 3.3GHz
4GB 1600MHz RAM
500GB 5400rpm hard drive
Intel HD Graphics 4000
NVIDIA GeForce GT 650M with
512MB of GDDR5 memory
1440 × 900 display
7 hour battery

at 1680 × 1050 pixels, and you can alternatively specify this resolution in a glossy screen. This is an interesting option, because it lets you fit a larger desktop on the 15in display without moving to Retina, which requires new ways of handling the relative sizing of user interface and content that not all apps are ready for yet.

Sum of its parts Compared to the Retina models, let alone the tiny Air, the MacBook Pro looks relatively chunky, but there are benefits to that. Aside from the inclusion of an optical drive, the use of a hard disk rather than solid state memory means you can get more gigabytes inside your laptop: the build-to-order options rise to a terabyte, and the price still isn't

scary, which can't be said of 1TB SSDs. If you do prefer SSD, though, that's an option too, with capacities from 128GB to 512GB available in both the 13in and 15in models. It's also quite feasible to get at the hard disk later to upgrade, repair or replace it, unlike with the sealed Retina and Air. You can even replace the battery yourself without a great deal of difficulty, although Apple says this will void your warranty. Various third-party upgrade kits are available for MacBook Pros, for example to swap out the optical drive so you can fit a hard disk and SSD at the same time.

All MacBook Pros are limited to a maximum of 8GB of RAM, and it's worth the £80 to get this at the start rather than the base 4GB; but the RAM is officially user-upgradable, so you could buy the extra chips and install them if you prefer.

Apple add-ons

Macs work with the same industry-standard accessories and peripherals as PCs, but Apple's own have some unique advantages.

Apple TV

Buy this affordable gadget, plug it into your HDTV set and connect it to your wifi network to put your Apple kit at the heart of your home. Access iTunes direct, play music and movies from your Mac, or send whatever's on your Mac or iPad screen to the TV with a tap.

↓ AirPort Time Capsule

An AirPort Extreme with a 2TB or 3TB hard disk built in. Use it as your router and wireless Time Machine backup drive in one. It can attach an extra USB hard drive or printer to your wifi network, too.

↑ AirPort Extreme

Redesigned to support 802.11ac, the latest higher-speed wifi standard, Apple's easy-to-use router is one of the most efficient and reliable ways to connect your Mac and other computers and devices to your broadband modem.

→ AirPort Express

Originally built into a mains plug unit, now a tiny standalone box similar to Apple TV, AirPort Express is an endlessly helpful networking aid. Convert wifi to Ethernet or vice versa; extend a network; receive digital audio streams and output them to analogue speakers; connect a USB-only printer or hard disk to your wired or wireless network; its uses are myriad. When you're not using it at home, slip it in your laptop bag to solve network niggles on the road.

↗ Thunderbolt Display

Designed for the new interface featured in all the latest Macs, this top-quality screen is the ideal desktop companion to a MacBook. (Other, cheaper, screens are available.)

↙ Magic Mouse

MacBooks have the best trackpads of any laptop – but it's still OK if you prefer a mouse! The Magic Mouse is also very fine, with a touch-sensitive surface for gestures, and connects wirelessly to your Mac.

→ Apple keyboards

The wired and wireless keyboards that come as standard with iMacs can also be bought separately. Many MacBook users invest so they can type more comfortably when at a desk, perhaps using a stand to prop the MacBook itself higher up, where the screen is easier to see. But you must make a choice: numeric keypad and wires, or wireless operation via Bluetooth and no keypad?

↗ USB SuperDrive

Now that most MacBook models don't have a built-in DVD drive, installing software from disc, burning a DVD for your grandma or accessing optical archives can be a challenge. The inexpensive Apple USB SuperDrive is the answer, providing the same hardware that isn't in your Mac in a stylish aluminium case, ready to plug in when you need it.

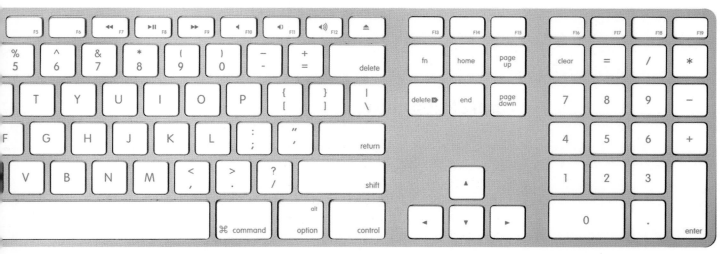

Chapter 2
OS X

The Mac desktop

Apple invented the graphical user interface as we know it, so OS X will feel familiar to any computer user. Let's take a closer look.

The Dock

The Dock runs across the bottom of the screen and gives you quick access to commonly used apps, documents and folders. The Mac's file browser, called the Finder, always has its icon in the first position at the left, and the Trash basket at the far right, but all the other icons can be moved around, deleted or added as you like.

You'll notice the Dock is split into two un-equal parts. The larger portion, at the left, shows all the apps that are currently running, indicated by a bluish-white light in the bar below, plus any apps that you choose to keep handy in the Dock permanently, which appear without the light when not running. If an app is in the process of launching or needs attention, it'll bounce repeatedly.

To the right of the Dock's dividing line sit other items that you want to remain visible. In addition to the Trash, your Documents and Downloads folders will appear here by default. Click either of them and its contents pop up in a fan; you can then click on any document in the fan to open it (or run it, if it's an app). If there are too

> ## MOVING FROM WINDOWS
>
> **OS X is the name of the Mac's operating system, pronounced 'oh ess ten'. It looks different from Windows, the operating system installed on most PCs, but they have many common features. Each uses windows to display things and a pointer to interact with them. Where Windows has the Taskbar at the foot of the screen, the Mac has the Dock. While Windows apps each have their own menu bar inside their own windows, OS X has one menu bar at the top of the screen, which changes when you switch between apps.**

many items in the fan to fit on the screen, click the ringed arrow at the top of the list.

Working with stacks

These sets of items are called stacks. You can change the way they

Finder   Launchpad   Mission Control   Other apps   *Drag any icon along the Dock to rearrange it*

display by right-clicking the icon. As in Windows, right-clicking most things on your Mac will pop up a contextual menu showing options specific to that item. In this case, the menu lets you choose whether this stack appears as a fan, a grid or a list, and how the items it shows will be sorted. Or you can let your Mac choose automatically depending on how big the stack is.

By default, when you switch on your Mac for the first time, the Dock icon for each stack is a little pile of documents, seen from the top, with the most recent item on top. That's sometimes handy, but makes it hard to see at a glance which is your Downloads folder, for example, so you may want to choose Folder instead of Stack in the contextual menu – then the icon will represent the type of folder you're looking at.

You can add any folder as a stack to make it quickly accessible in future. Make sure you're in the Finder: the current app is named at the top left of the screen, the only bold menu heading. If you're not, click the Finder icon at the left of the Dock. Now hold the Cmd key (the Mac's equiv-

↑ **Folders that are listed at the right-hand end of the Dock can be displayed in various ways.**

alent of Ctrl in Windows; the Ctrl key on a Mac serves different purposes) and press 'N' to open a new window. By default, every Finder window has a sidebar on the left listing commonly used storage locations on your system. Let's add the Applications folder, which normally stores all the programs on your Mac, to the Dock, to make it easy to find apps whose icons aren't in the Dock.

Near the top of the sidebar you'll see your Mac's main hard disk (startup drive), normally labelled Macintosh HD. Click this once to view its contents in the main part of the window at the right. Near the top you'll see the Applications folder. Drag it across the screen to the Dock and hold it there at the left of the Trash icon. Notice how the other stacks shuffle along to make space for it. Let go when it's positioned where you want it, and it'll move smartly into place. Its icon either shows a pile of apps, or the Applications folder icon (like an 'A'), depending on your stack options.

If you accidentally drop the Applications folder somewhere else – for example, onto another Finder window – the Finder may start copying its contents to that location. Don't panic: see 'Help, I got it wrong' on the next page.

THE RIGHT WAY TO CLICK

Years ago, Mac mice had only one button, so to right-click you held the Ctrl key. This still works, but you can also right-click on your MacBook by tapping the trackpad with two fingers. Alternatives are available in the Trackpad pane of System Preferences. Or you can plug in an Apple Magic Mouse, or any other USB mouse, and right-click, just like in Windows.

Folders   *Trash*

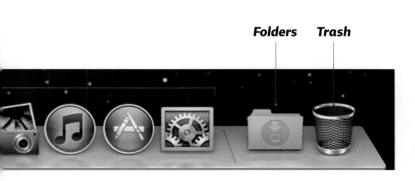

HELP, I GOT IT WRONG

If you put any process in motion on your Mac by accident, you can generally stop it by hitting Cmd-. (that is, hold the Cmd key and press the full stop or period key). For example, if a box pops up saying it's copying 100 files, and you hadn't meant to do that, hit Cmd-. and everything will stay just as it was. If you've already made a mistake, hit Cmd-Z straight away to undo it. These shortcuts will save a lot of hassle.

Adding and removing apps

Apple includes some essential apps in the Dock for you, including Safari, the Mac's default web browser – but you can rearrange or remove them, or add others. Click the Applications icon near the top of the sidebar in any Finder window to see all your installed apps, then drag any one to the Dock and drop it where you want it. If you change your mind and want to remove it, right-click the Dock icon and choose Options > Remove from Dock (this isn't possible if the app is currently running).

Tweaking the Dock

To make the Dock bigger (to see icons more clearly) or smaller (to fit more icons in), hover over the dividing line to the left of the Trash icon and your stacks, so that the cursor turns into a double-headed arrow, then drag up or down. You can adjust the Dock's appearance and behaviour further: either right-click in the same place, or click the Apple icon at the top left of the screen to show the Apple menu, then pick Dock. Extra options are found in the Dock Preferences submenu here.

The Trash

Whenever you delete something on your Mac – for example, by selecting a file in the Finder and pressing Cmd-Backspace – it normally ends up in the Trash. To see what's in the

Trash, click the Trash icon in the Dock (it always opens as a folder in a new window). To resurrect a deleted file, right-click it and choose Put Back, or drag the file to where you want it stored.

If you let deleted files build up in the Trash, it won't have any bad effect, but they'll take up disk space. Now and again, right-click the Trash icon and pick Empty Trash. If the deleted files include confidential information, hold the Cmd key and the option changes to Secure Empty Trash. Select this to delete the files permanently, with no hope of retrieving them using unerase software later, but little or no risk of others doing so either.

← **Deleted files aren't erased until you empty the Trash, and only Secure Empty prevents later recovery.**

↑ **The Apple menu is always available, regardless of which app you're currently using.**

The Mac menu bar

OS X's menu bar runs across the top of the screen at all times, unless you're using an app in full-screen mode or one that takes over the display completely, such as a game. Every app, even the Finder, uses the same menu bar, but each will display its own submenus and commands in it.

↑ At the right-hand end of the menu bar you'll find tools including search and status icons.

Like the Dock, the menu bar has two parts. At the left side of the screen, the Apple menu (which never changes) is always followed by a menu labelled in bold with the name of the app you're currently using; this always contains that app's Preferences and options to hide or quit it. The app's other menus then follow.

At the far right of the menu bar is an icon to show or hide Notification Center, a relatively new feature of OS X that lets you keep up to date with reminders, updates, alerts and social media while you work. To the left of this is a magnifying glass icon representing Spotlight, OS X's system-wide search facility. After these, you'll find utility icons similar to those found in Windows' 'system tray', including the clock, your Mac's battery level and network connection status, and various other optional tools – for example, to set the volume and screen resolution. Clicking any of these icons drops down a menu related to it.

| **Apple menu** | The Apple menu at the top left of the screen gives you access to important tools for managing |

SEE MORE

Hold the Alt key (labelled Alt, although Apple still officially calls it Option) while clicking a menu bar icon and you'll often see additional information in its menu.

---

your Mac – although most of them can also be accessed from elsewhere. The first, About This Mac, pops up a simple box reminding you what version of OS X you're running and what processor (CPU) and how much memory your Mac has. You won't normally need to use the Software Update button here, because by default OS X will tell you automatically when any updates are available; it's usually a good idea to install these when invited to, especially those that relate to security. In OS X 10.8 Mountain Lion and later, Software Update is integrated with the Mac App Store and will alert you to updates via Notification Center.

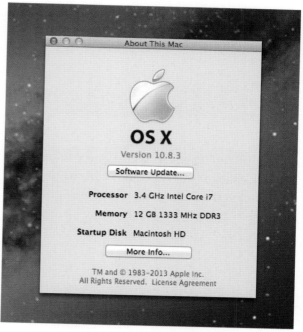

↑ About This Mac lists basic attributes of your system, but click More Info for the full details.

| **Sleep, Restart, Shut Down** | Your Mac will put itself to sleep after a period of inactivity, controlled in your Energy Saver preferences, which we'll cover later in this book. While sleep- |

ing (indicated by a 'breathing' LED on its case), your MacBook will use very little battery power, but if necessary it'll automatically put itself into a deeper sleep, from which it'll take a few extra seconds to wake. There's generally no reason to use the Shut Down command.

← **System Preferences can be accessed from the Apple menu or from the Dock, where its icon shows a set of cogs. It presents most of the settings for your Mac in one place. Click once on any icon to open a dedicated pane for that aspect of your system.**

If your Mac is behaving oddly – for example, things are gradually slowing down, or an app crashes every time you open it – you can try rebooting it using Restart. Selecting this command brings up a box that asks you to confirm or cancel, but note that if you do nothing, the system *will* restart after one minute. Mountain Lion has the ability to reopen all your apps and windows after a restart (or shutdown) so everything's just as you left it, but non-Apple apps may not support this, so save your work before restarting. If you haven't, the app should warn you and halt the restart.

The final command on the Apple menu, Log Out, leaves the Mac switched on but logs you out of your user account, so anyone who comes along can't use it without your password. That's if you've set up a password: we'll explain how to manage user accounts on your Mac later in this book.

Recent Items

Often overlooked, the Recent Items submenu on the Apple menu lists apps, files and remote servers (if any) that you've recently used, and is a handy way to find them again. A related feature is the Recent Places list you'll see if you click the file location drop-down menu at the top of any app's Open or Save box.

Force quit

Although today's Macs tend to run smoothly and crashes are rare, sometimes an app will get itself in a mess. You'll know because it stops responding while you're using it (and doesn't pop back into life after you give it a minute) or refuses to come to the foreground when you try to switch to it. The last resort is to force it to quit. Right-click the app's Dock icon and hold the Alt key to change the Quit option to Force Quit, then choose this and wait for the app to die, usually with a plaintive error report box. Alternatively, choose Force Quit from the Apple menu to see a list of currently running apps, then pick the one you want to kill. The same list can be displayed by pressing Cmd-Alt-Esc at any time. Note that the Finder is an app, and if you notice other apps struggling to perform file operations, for example, it may be the Finder that's crashed. It's easy to tell: right-click its Dock icon and it'll give you the option to 'relaunch'.

Running apps

Your Mac can run many apps at the same time, and OS X has several features to make that more convenient and less confusing.

Switching between apps

Even if you've only been using your Mac a few minutes, you'll probably see a handful of 'lights' at the bottom of the Dock showing that apps are active. Within reason, it's rarely necessary to quit apps; OS X will prioritise those that you're actually using over those that are idle, so you shouldn't see any loss of performance except

↑ **Hold Cmd while repeatedly tapping Tab to flip quickly between currently running apps.**

an occasional pause when switching to an app you haven't used for a while. But your Mac may feel more responsive when you turn off some of those lights by quitting apps, especially if you're using heavyweight software and handling large files.

Assuming you do have several apps open, you can switch from the one you're currently using to another by clicking its icon in the Dock, but a much quicker way is to hold down the Cmd key and press Tab. Keep your thumb on Cmd to see a bar (known as a bezel) across the middle of the screen showing the icons of all the apps currently running. Making this list manageably short is

another reason to quit apps you're not busy with. Continue tapping Tab until you get to the app you want (hold Shift while tapping Tab to step backwards if you overshoot), then release Cmd to switch to that app. Or, while holding Cmd to keep the bezel visible, you can also click an app within it using the mouse pointer. Tapping Cmd-Tab once always goes back to the last app you were in, so you can flip back and forth quickly.

You can also quit apps from the bezel. With Cmd still held down, tap Q to quit the selected app.

Notice that you can switch between apps while you're dragging. Start dragging a picture in Safari, say; keep your finger on the mouse button while you Cmd-Tab over to TextEdit; then drop the picture into the document you're working on.

KINDS OF MEMORY

Apps, documents and other files are stored permanently on your Mac's hard drive (whether it's a mechanical disk or an SSD, based on flash memory). When you run an app or open a document, it's copied into memory (RAM), where the processor (CPU) can access it. But to enable you to keep more apps and documents open than your Mac's RAM can hold, OS X uses a temporary area of the hard drive to store some of the data, swapping it in and out of RAM as required. This is invisible to the user until things start to get clogged.

↑ Mission Control zooms you out to show all the windows of the active apps. Scroll on any stack (two-finger swipe up on your trackpad) to enlarge its windows. Click any window to go to it.

Mission Control

Different apps will each have their own windows, often several of them for multiple documents, and all of these can appear on the screen simultaneously, overlapping each other. This can make it hard to see the window you want. One way to impose order is to use the Hide commands in the Application menu (the one next to the Apple logo) to hide an app you're not using or hide everything except the app you *are* using. You can still switch to a hidden app, via the Dock or the bezel, and its windows will instantly become visible again.

A more sophisticated approach is to press the F3 key or click the Mission Control icon in the Dock. This zooms out your desktop and separates out all the windows, a feature previously known as Exposé. You can also launch it by swiping upwards with three fingers on your MacBook trackpad, or by double-tapping with two fingers on a Magic Mouse. Or press Cmd-F3 to spread out just the windows of the current app, so they don't overlap. Tap the same shortcut to return to normal, or click any window you can see to zoom back into that. Press Alt-F3 to adjust Mission Control's options.

ON THE BIG SCREEN

Some apps, such as Safari and iTunes, have the option to run in a full-screen mode. Look for the diagonal arrows icon at the top right of the app's window. Clicking this is different from just maximising an app window to fill the screen: the Mac menu bar disappears, only returning temporarily if you move the pointer to the top of the screen.

Working with desktops

At the top of the Mission Control screen you'll see two or more thumbnail screens. These represent the Dashboard, your desktop(s), and any apps you're running in full-screen mode. You can add extra desktops by clicking the panel labelled with a plus sign (+) that appears when you go to the top right of the screen. When you go to

← The Dashboard comes with several useful Widgets for a variety of purposes. You can remove ones you don't need by clicking the minus sign, or install more by clicking the plus sign. Like apps, Widgets can be made by others as well as Apple.

Dashboard Widgets

Widgets are tiny apps that work in single fixed-size windows within the Dashboard, a separate space within OS X. Go to it by pressing F4, or use the shortcuts mentioned above to flip to it via Mission Control. You can move Widgets around the screen as you like, or click the minus sign at the bottom left to show a cross on each Widget that you can click to remove it from the Dashboard. The Widget is just hidden, not deleted; you'll still see it if you click the plus sign to show all your Widgets as app icons. You can then click More Widgets to find extra ones online.

Clicking a Widget's window may switch between different display modes, or there may be an 'i' symbol you can click to flip it over, showing extra options on the 'back' of the window.

→ Launchpad shows apps as icons, like on an iPad.

any one of your desktops, you can then arrange apps, Finder windows and so on as you please within it – a feature previously known as Spaces.

It can be useful to have one space for your day job, one for a side project, one for the album you're mixing in your spare time, and so on; you can switch instantly between setups via Mission Control.

Another way to switch between spaces is to drag left or right with three fingers on your trackpad (or with two on a Magic Mouse). You can do the same by holding Ctrl and tapping the left or right cursor key.

Spotlight

Apple's handy system-wide search tool can be used not only to hunt for files, but to find and launch apps, and a great deal more.

Searching your Mac

Click the magnifying glass icon at the top right of the screen, or press Cmd-Space, to open the Spotlight search box at any time. You can start typing straight away, and as soon as you do, Spotlight starts showing results, continually refining them as you type. These results are drawn from all parts of your Mac's file system, including folder names, documents, spreadsheets, images, apps, emails, and even web pages you've recently visited.

You can move through the list of results using the cursor arrow keys, or just click an item to highlight it; it's then previewed in a pop-up pane to the left. To open the item itself, press Return. Alternatively, if the item is a document, hold Cmd

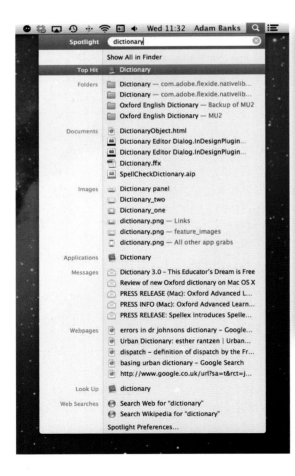

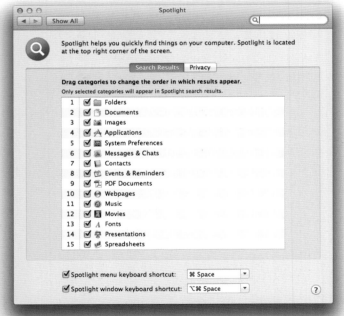

↑ **Use Spotlight's pane in System Preferences to choose what kinds of files to find and (in the Privacy tab) which locations not to search.**

← **Spotlight makes it easy to find anything anywhere on your system, including external storage, just by typing part of its name into the box.**

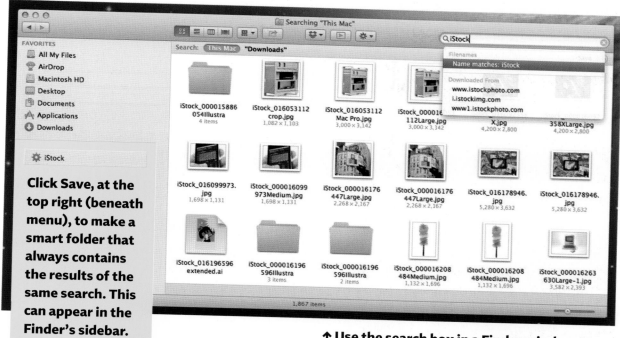

Click Save, at the top right (beneath menu), to make a smart folder that always contains the results of the same search. This can appear in the Finder's sidebar.

↑ **Use the search box in a Finder window to search your whole Mac or just this folder. Click '+' (just seen, top right) to add criteria.**

while clicking it or pressing Return to open the folder that contains it in a Finder window.

If there are too many results to see, click Show All in Finder to open a regular Finder window showing all the files (including web pages, emails and so on) that match your requirements.

Taming Spotlight

If you find you're always seeing certain kinds of items in Spotlight that you don't need, or it's searching locations that will never be relevant (such as a backup drive), you can tell it what *not* to find.

WORK IT OUT!

As well as finding files, Spotlight can find answers. Type 2+2 and the search result will be 4. Enter 2*3 and you'll get 6. For 20/(10*4) the result is 0.5, while sqrt(9*4) gives 6, the square root of 36. 6^2 means 6 to the power of 2, which is 36. And 50*20% returns a result of 10, 20% of 50.

Open System Preferences from the Dock or the Apple menu, and click Spotlight. Untick any file types you don't want. You can also change the order in which results will appear in Spotlight by dragging categories up and down the list. By default, applications appear first, which makes Spotlight a handy way to launch apps without looking through the Dock. Just hit Cmd-Space, start typing the name of an app, and press Return.

In the Privacy tab, you can exclude specified storage locations from searches. Click the plus sign to add folders or drives that you *don't* want to search. If Spotlight ever fails to work properly, try adding your Macintosh HD here, then removing it.

Finder searches

A Spotlight search box also appears at the top right of any Finder window. After typing a search term here, you can choose (at far left) whether to search your whole Mac or just the current folder. At the top right, click the plus sign to add search criteria, and Save to make your search a 'smart folder', which will always contain current results for that search.

Accessibility

Helpful features make sure everyone can use OS X comfortably, even if the trackpad, keyboard or display present difficulties.

Accessibility Preferences

Open System Preferences (from the Apple menu or the Dock) and click Accessibility. This pane lets you tweak many aspects of OS X's user interface, categorised under Seeing, Hearing and Interacting. These changes will apply to all apps that work in the standard OS X way.

Perhaps the most important enhancement Apple offers for visually impaired users is VoiceOver, which speaks the names of on-screen elements as you select them or pass over them with the mouse pointer. Having selected VoiceOver in the left panel, click Open VoiceOver Utility for a huge range of options. Click Speech, then click the drop-down menu under Voice and pick Customize to see the wide range of voices available. 'Daniel' is the same voice that's used for Siri on the iPhone and other iOS devices in the UK; British users can also choose 'Emily' or 'Serena', and dozens of other options are here for international languages and dialects. VoiceOver's output can also be redirected to a Braille display if you have one connected to your MacBook.

In Accessibility's Audio settings, users with hearing difficulties can opt to flash the screen when an alert would usually make a noise.

Many of OS X's accessibility features will be useful to all users, regardless of disability. For example, double-tap with two fingers on your MacBook's trackpad (or one finger on a Magic Mouse) to zoom into a Safari window.

You can zoom in many additional ways by turning on options in Accessibility Pref-

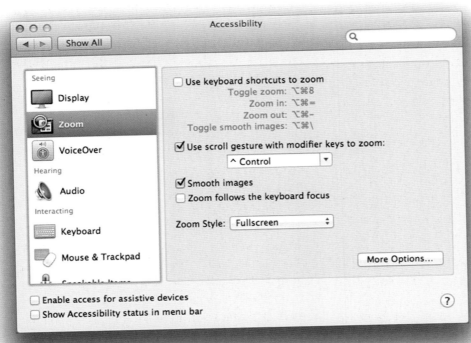

↑ The Accessibility pane in System Preferences offers alternative ways to interact with your Mac, including support for accessibility devices.

→ Dictation lets you speak what you want to write instead of typing it. Based on your language, OS X will do a fair job of transcribing your words, looking at data such as your contacts to help it figure out what you meant to say.

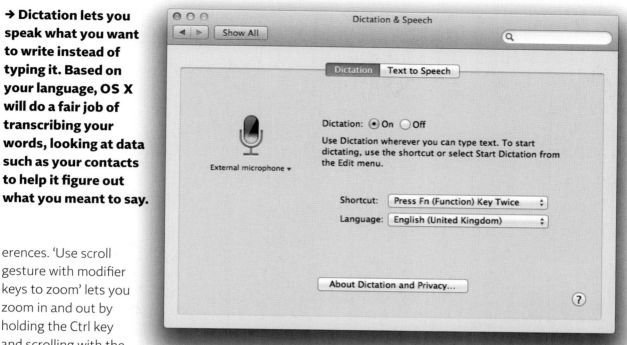

erences. 'Use scroll gesture with modifier keys to zoom' lets you zoom in and out by holding the Ctrl key and scrolling with the trackpad or mouse (as in previous versions of OS X), or you can activate zoom shortcuts based on the plus, minus and asterisk keys.

Dictation   Software such as Dragon Dictate is available for Macs if you need advanced dictation and voice command features, but Apple

↓ If the standard display isn't easy for you to read, you can adjust contrast, invert colours, switch to black-and-white, or enlarge the cursor (mouse pointer). Don't forget the F1 and F2 keys also control screen brightness.

has now built a basic and actually quite capable dictation facility into OS X. It works similarly to Siri's dictation in iOS, and even uses the same purple microphone icon as Siri. You'll need to turn it on in the Dictation & Speech pane of System Preferences. Like Siri, it'll only work if you have a live broadband connection, since the processing is done on Apple's servers. You're warned that this also means your speech and personal information will be transmitted over the internet, although this shouldn't present any significant privacy risk.

To dictate into an app, put your text cursor where you want to start and double-tap the activation key set in Dictation & Speech (Fn by default). Then just start talking. Your MacBook's built-in microphone (or dual microphones in recent models, helping to isolate your voice) should pick up your speech without any trouble, although if you dictate regularly with a background of office noise you might need to try a pair of iPhone earbuds, with their inline mic, or a third-party wired or Bluetooth headset.

Click Done when you've finished, and a few moments later the transcribed text will appear in your document. In our tests, Dictation was about 95% accurate, despite not requiring any 'training' – but that still leaves quite a few mistakes to fix.

User accounts

You can set up your Mac with just one user who has access to everything, but it often makes sense to create alternative logins.

Account privileges

Open the Users & Groups pane of System Preferences and you'll see all the user accounts that exist for your Mac in the list at the left. To make any changes to this, you'll need to click the lock icon below and enter the password for an administrator account. If you only have one user account set up, it'll be an administrator. When you add others, however, you can limit what those users can do. So if you log in as you, you'll have full access to all your Mac's settings and can add, delete, install and so forth at will (though you'll still be asked for your password before performing security-critical operations); but before you allow someone else to use the Mac, you can log out, then give them a login that grants them lesser privileges. It's essential if you'll be sharing your Mac with other users to whom you don't want to completely entrust your system.

It's also a handy way to allow each user to have the Mac set up just the way they want it. When you install apps or services or change settings, they're typically specific to the current user, although some are system-wide and some give you a choice. Within the Users folder on your main hard drive (Macintosh HD), OS X keeps a separate folder for each user account. The currently active user is labelled with a little house. If you're an Admin, you can see the contents of all these folders, but Standard users (which just means those for whom you haven't ticked 'Allow user to administer this computer' when setting up their account) can

↑ **Your first user must be an administrator, but when you create others you can make them Standard, Managed or Guest accounts instead.**

only see inside their own home folders; the others will appear empty except for a Public folder. Any user can access files in another's Public folder, and make copies of them, but can't modify or delete them. Nor can they add files to someone else's Public folder, but inside each Public folder is a Drop Box folder, into which others can drag files that they want to pass to that user.

Parental Controls

If you really want to limit what a particular user can do, tick the option to enable parental controls, then click Open Parental Controls. (The separate Parental Controls item in System Preferences brings you to the same place.) Here you can limit what apps the user can run, individually or, for Mac App Store titles, by age rating; who they can email and message; and even at what times of the day or week they're allowed access to the Mac. The Web tab is quite honest about the limitations of internet filtering – '*Try* to limit access to adult websites' is the best any system can promise – but also lets you specify sites that should and shouldn't be shown, or limit web access to just a list of approved sites.

You can also view a log of websites this user has recently visited. If you don't like what you see, you can immediately block any site; or if you'd rather forget what you've seen, right-click the log title at the left and choose 'Clear log history'. Logs are also available for apps and messages. Consider the privacy implications before applying Parental Controls to users other than your children.

Switching accounts

User accounts are only of value if you're rigorous about logging out of your own Admin account when you're not sitting at your Mac – otherwise others can come along and use it logged in as you. Click Login Options at the bottom left of Users & Groups and you'll see the Automatic Login option. Chances are this is ticked, so OS X is logging you in without asking. Set this to Off, and whenever the Mac is started up or woken from sleep (you can set how fast it falls asleep in the Energy Saver

↑ **The default Guest account, which anyone can log in to without a password, lets house guests access but not administer the system, and deletes their folder once they leave.**

↑ **Enabling Parental Controls lets you apply a range of specific limits to a user's activity.**

pane of System Preferences) it'll ask for a login. You can opt to show a 'fast user switching' menu at the right of the menu bar, which constantly displays the username of the account currently logged in and lets you quickly flip to a different one – if you have the password for it.

Backing up your files

A wide variety of third-party backup products and services are available, but for most users OS X's built-in Time Machine is ideal.

Using Time Machine

The data on your Mac may be your most valuable possession. From work files to family photos, if it disappeared it could be impossible to replace. So you really need a foolproof backup system in place to ensure you always have a separate copy.

Time Machine is a feature of OS X that maintains a rolling backup of your Mac's main hard drive (and connected drives, if you choose) on a connected external drive, without you even having to think about it. By storing changes in a clever way, it can use a drive about the same size as the one you're backing up to duplicate not only what's on that drive now, but everything that's been on it for months, letting you roll back the whole drive or, more usefully, any individual file or folder to any point in the past. It keeps a backup from every hour in the past day, every day in the past month, and every week in the past… well, however long it can manage before the drive you're using fills up. Unless your hard disk is very full or your backup drive significantly smaller, expect well over a year. Older backups are then automatically ditched.

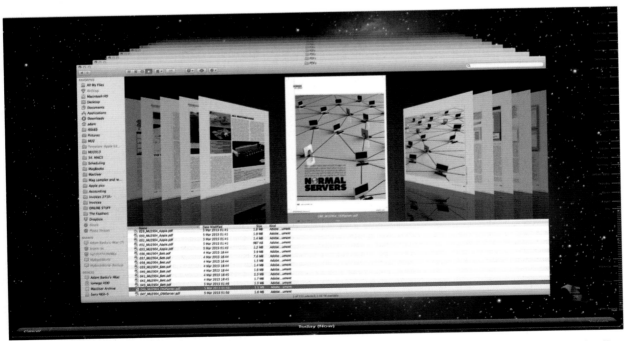

↑ **Time Machine lets you track any file back through the regular backups that have automatically been made of it over time, or look back within a folder to find an old file that's been deleted.**

Time Machine is generally reliable, and the ability to go back to any past instance of a file should be a great weight off your mind – well worth the cost of a hard drive. The only reason you might not be able to find exactly the file you want is if you created and then deleted it, or changed it repeatedly, in a short time, so Time Machine doesn't have a snapshot at just the right point. In most cases, though, you'll find something close to what you need.

To set up Time Machine, first plug in a suitable external hard disk or SSD. It must be in HFS+ format (the standard for Mac drives). Or you could use Apple's wifi Time Capsule drive, or a compatible NAS box from another maker.

Then go to Time Machine in System Preferences, turn the big switch to On and select that disk. If you have other drives too, click Options to choose which get backed up.

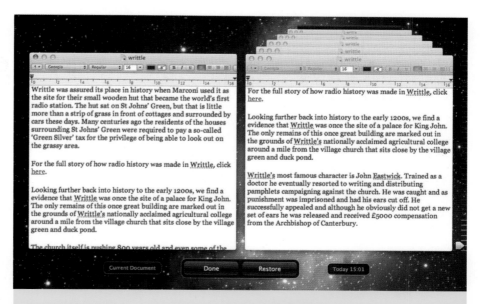

VERSIONS

Another way OS X protects your files is through versioning. Unlike Time Machine, this only works with compatible apps (mainly Apple apps at the moment). The idea is that your Mac watches for you taking a pause, then quietly saves a copy of the document you're working on. If nothing goes awry you can ignore this, but it's building up a trail of changes that you can work back through later if you forget to save your work, have a power cut or other disaster, or just realise you liked an earlier edit better.

Once you've saved a file in an app such as TextEdit, hovering the mouse pointer over its name in the title bar reveals a tiny triangle at the right. Click this to pop down a menu that includes the option to 'Browse all versions'. This leads to a Time Machine-style interface showing the document's current state on the left, with previous versions stacked up on the right. You can roll back through them by clicking on their headers or scrolling the timeline. It's easy to compare each version against the current one side by side.

Having found the version you want, click Restore and the Versions interface will gracefully slide away, leaving you to continue working on that version.

From now on, to invoke Time Machine, either have the document you want to roll back open in an Apple app (this won't work with third-party apps), or select it or open its enclosing folder in a Finder window. Click the Time Machine icon near the right of the Mac menu bar and choose Enter Time Machine. You're whisked into space, where you can flip between all the backed-up versions of this file. Find the one you want (press Cmd-Y, as in the Finder, to get a Quick Look preview of the file's contents, if OS X can read it) and click Restore, then choose whether to keep both this and the current version or just one.

You can even invoke Time Machine from Mail. Restored emails will appear under On My Mac > Time Machine in Mail's left sidebar.

Networking your Mac

Connecting to a router is the easiest way to share files with other computers around your home or office, and to get on the internet.

Router choices
There's nothing complicated about a basic network: all it need consist of is an ADSL modem with a built-in router, providing wifi access and three or four Ethernet ports to which you can connect Macs and PCs. The router plugs into your phone line for broadband internet. If you subscribe to a cable broadband service instead, you'll be provided with a cable modem and will need to add a separate wifi router.

The MacBook Air and Retina MacBook Pro don't have Ethernet ports – they're too skinny for this clunky old interface to fit – but Apple sells adaptors to convert a USB, FireWire or Thunderbolt port to Ethernet. Alternatively, it's more convenient and for most purposes just as effective to connect via wifi. Apple, which pioneered the inclusion of wifi in notebook computers, still

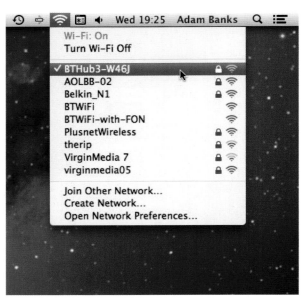

↑ **Connecting to a wifi network is just a matter of selecting the router in the Mac menu bar.**

PROTECT YOUR NETWORK

When you set up your router, be sure to set a WPA2 password. Routers protected by this or other security schemes (WPA2 is the only one you should use now) will show a lock icon when listed on your Mac and won't allow anyone to connect without the password. Without this feature, anyone could log on to your network and get at whatever files you're sharing, or more likely use your broadband to download copyright-infringing adult films.

refers to this feature by its own brand name, AirPort, but OS X (like iOS) has shifted towards the industry standard term Wi-Fi. Macs generally work with all the same wifi products as PCs.

Apple sells its own wifi router, the AirPort Extreme, which is worth considering (it doesn't include an ADSL modem, so you'll need a separate modem whether you're on ADSL or cable). Many ISPs offer you a router when you sign up, but they're often rubbish. Read magazine reviews of 802.11n routers to pick a decent one. Older 802.11g products will work with 802.11n, but they'll slow the whole network down, so try to stick to 802.11n. The next generation, 802.11ac, is already looming.

Why bother with Ethernet? Well, although the 100Mbit/sec interface on older devices is no faster in practice than modern wifi with good reception, the Gigabit Ethernet ports on today's Macs and routers are ten times faster, and still well ahead of any wireless connection. So it may be worth the hassle of connecting with Ethernet cables if you're regularly transferring a lot of data. But bear in mind it's unlikely to make access to the internet any faster, since your broadband connection is most likely to be the bottleneck.

You can also buy routers that connect to 3G rather than landlines, enabling you to access a cell network connection from your Mac and share it between computers and devices. You'll need a data tariff, but it's a useful option if you can't install wired broadband where you live or work, or need to connect multiple devices on the move.

REMOTE SERVERS

To connect to a remote server from your Mac, go to the Finder and press Cmd-K, then enter the server's IP address with a suitable prefix, such as smb://. Press Cmd-, (comma) to open Finder Preferences and make sure 'Connected servers' is ticked; servers you're connected to will then appear in the sidebar of Finder windows, after local storage.

WIFI ON THE MENU

Save time by displaying your wifi status in the Mac menu bar. This shows the strength of your connection at a glance, and lets you connect to new networks without using System Preferences. If the wifi icon (a series of radiating lines, or, if you're not connected, an empty pie segment) isn't visible near the right of the menu bar, go to the Network pane in System Preferences, select Wi-Fi and tick 'Show Wi-Fi status on menu bar'.

Connecting at home

Click the wifi logo near the right-hand end of the menu bar at the top of the screen, choose Turn Wi-Fi On if it's not already on, then select your router from the list. Each radiating beam of the wifi logo will be either black or grey to indicate the strength of the connection. If you can't get a strong signal from your router, try moving it, or consider an alternative such as powerline networking, which sends data through your mains electrical wiring: you just plug in an adaptor next to your router and another next to your Mac, and connect them up. Or if it's practical, connect your Mac's Ethernet port directly to one of the router's LAN sockets.

You shouldn't need to do anything further to access the internet via your router, which should be set to automatically allocate the IP addresses that each computer needs, using DHCP (Dynamic Host Configuration Protocol). If you ever need to check your Mac's IP address, perhaps so that you can connect to it remotely or to diagnose conflicts, check System Preferences > Network. Select the interface you're using on the left (Wi-Fi or Ethernet) and on the right you'll see its connection status and, if connected, its IP address.

If you can't seem to get connected, or are connected but can't access the internet in Safari, Mail and so on, you may need to contact your broadband provider, but turning the modem and router off and on again will often work wonders.

Sharing files

To enable other Macs on your network to access files on yours, go to Sharing in System Preferences, tick File Sharing, and with this option highlighted take note of which drives and folders are listed on the right. You can edit who has access to what: pick Everyone if you're having trouble (only users who have access to your network can share anyway).

The easiest way to find one Mac on your network from another is using Bonjour, Apple's way of making networking foolproof. In the Finder, choose Preferences from the Finder menu and make sure 'Bonjour computers' is ticked. Any

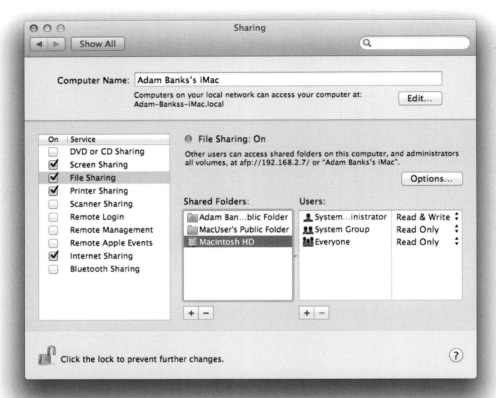

← **To allow other Macs and PCs on your own network to access files on your Mac, set up Sharing in System Preferences. When you add a drive or folder to the list of Shared Folders, the permissions shown at the right apply to all folders within this, except those you add separately and give their own permissions.**

Macs set to share should then appear in the sidebar of any Finder window, under Sharing.

Sharing with PCs

Macs are quite happy to network with Windows PCs too, but setting up file sharing is slightly more complicated. Go to the PC you want to access from your Mac and find out its IP address: hold the Windows key and press R, then type ncpa.cpl into the box that appears. Press Return to see current network connections, then double-click the active connection, click Details and find the IP address in the listing that appears.

Go back to your Mac, and in the Finder press Cmd-K to open the Connect to Server dialog box. Type smb:// followed by the IP address you just found, which should be in the form of four numbers separated by full stops. When asked, enter the name and password for a valid user account on that PC (you may need to ask the owner of the PC if you didn't set it up yourself). Choose which volume you want to mount. Once you're connected, the PC should appear in the sidebar of any Finder window for easy access.

Now the opposite case: accessing files on your Mac from a PC. On the Mac, click Options in the File Sharing pane of System Preferences and tick 'Share files and folders using SMB (Windows)'. Also make sure the user account whose files you want to share is ticked; you'll need to enter the user account password to do this.

Make sure you know the full name of this user account (listed as 'Full name' in System Preferences > Users & Groups) *and* the short name, as seen on your home folder inside Users or in the Finder sidebar. On the PC, press the Windows key and enter 'credential manager'. Press Return to go to this. Click to add a Windows credential and add the IP address of your Mac, your Mac account name and its password. Once you've clicked OK in this dialog, you won't have to enter them again to connect to the Mac later.

Finally, select Computer from the Windows Start menu and click the 'Map network drive' button on the toolbar. Choose a drive letter to use (such as Y) and enter the IP address of your Mac and its home folder name. That user folder will be mounted as a drive under the Computer section of the Windows Explorer sidebar.

Connecting on the go

Wherever you take your MacBook, you'll probably need internet access. Follow our tips to get online wherever you find yourself.

Network settings are found in the Network pane of System Preferences. A quick way to open it is at the foot of the wifi menu in the Mac menu bar.

Specifying a service order

Your MacBook has several ways to connect to the internet built in, including wifi, Bluetooth and possibly Ethernet and FireWire, and you may have other options available, such as business VPNs or a smartphone. This means your Network sidebar can become quite a muddle. Does it matter? Well, when trying to establish a connection, OS X will work through the interfaces in the order listed. So it's worth making sure the one you prefer appears at the top of the list. This will make sure OS X doesn't latch on to one that might cost you money – a tethered iPhone connection, say – or is less effective, when a better option is available. Click the cog icon below the list and pick Set Service Order. Drag entries up or down, then click OK to apply your changes.

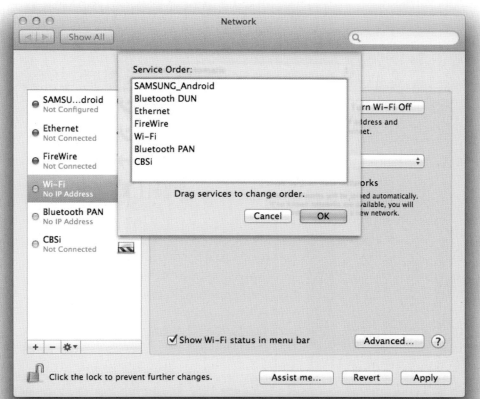

← **The Network Preferences pane lists all your network interfaces on the left, flagged with their current status. Arranging the list in order of preference – usually with Ethernet or wifi at the top – will help to ensure your MacBook connects quickly and successfully to the most appropriate service, wherever you are.**

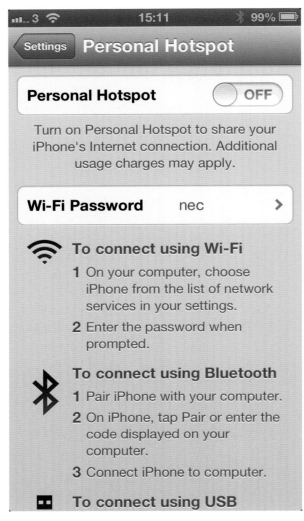

↑ Set up a Personal Hotspot on your iPhone or cellular iPad and your MacBook can get online.

Using a tethered connection

If wifi isn't available where you are, an alternative way to get your MacBook onto the internet is to share the 3G data connection of an iPhone or cellular iPad. (You may also be able to do this with a non-Apple smartphone or tablet.) This is known as tethering, and most network providers require you to take a special tariff for it, and/or charge extra for the data used. This may seem illogical – after all, it's still you accessing the internet from the same account – but a Mac tends to consume data faster than an iPhone, partly because content downloaded or streamed to a big screen is likely to be in a higher-bandwidth format.

Go to Settings on your iOS device, tap Personal Hotspot and enable the service to get started. You now have three options for using the shared connection with your MacBook.

In many ways, the most sensible is to connect the device's supplied Lightning or Dock connector to a USB port on your MacBook, enabling it to charge from the Mac's battery, reducing the chance you'll lose your connection when the iOS device runs out of juice. Once connected this way, open Network Preferences on your MacBook and select iPhone as the connection interface.

If you prefer to tether without wires, you can use Bluetooth, but you'll first need to pair the iOS device with your MacBook. Open the Bluetooth pane in System Preferences on your Mac, click the plus sign at the bottom and enable Bluetooth, if it's not already switched on. It will now start hunting for Bluetooth devices within range. Make sure Bluetooth is also enabled on your iPhone or iPad (in Settings > Bluetooth). OS X will provide a code number that you'll need to accept on your iOS device to pair them. You can now use the Bluetooth interface in Network Preferences to get online through your iPhone.

Finally, you can connect via wifi. Your iPhone will create a new wireless network called iPhone, which you can pick from the list of available networks on your Mac. You'll need the wifi password given on the Personal Hotspot setup screen.

↑ Bluetooth pairing should be painless.

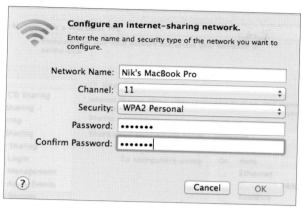

Configure an internet–sharing network.
Enter the name and security type of the network you want to configure.

Network Name: Nik's MacBook Pro
Channel: 11
Security: WPA2 Personal
Password: ••••••
Confirm Password: ••••••

Cancel   OK

↑ If your Mac can get online but your wifi devices can't, share your internet connection.

Sharing a wired connection

When you're travelling or visiting work premises, you may sometimes find your MacBook *can* get on the internet, using an Ethernet socket, but your iOS devices can't, since there's no wifi. The solution is the opposite of tethering: sharing the Mac's internet connection.

Go to the Sharing pane in System Preferences and click Internet Sharing. You won't be able to enable it until you specify how the connection should be shared, so use the drop-down list to select Ethernet as the interface from which you're sharing, and Wi-Fi below as the secondary interface through which others will access the service.

Now tick Internet Sharing in the sidebar to activate it. OS X will warn you that you could interfere with the operation of the network (well, so could many things!) and that you need to be connected to mains power. If you're OK with both of those caveats, click Start. Your MacBook will create a new wifi network, using its name as the SSID – the network name that appears in lists of available wifi connections. This will show up on other devices, which can then connect, indicated on your Mac by the wifi icon on your menu bar becoming a solid cone with an upward arrow.

There's no security by default, so your free wifi access point is likely to be colonised by guests in nearby hotel rooms, fellow passengers on your train or whatever. Better to click Wi-Fi Options at the bottom, select WPA2 Personal as the security type and enter a new password. Don't use your Mac Admin password, because you don't want to be giving that out to friends and colleagues.

Defining locations

Apple recognises that you'll need to connect to different networks in different places, and they may have their own unique configurations. Most routers will have DHCP (Dynamic Host Configuration Protocol) active, so connection will be simple and automatic, but some might require you to enter details such as an IP address. To save you having to re-enter these each time, OS X lets you set up 'locations' – discrete configuration profiles for each network, which you can switch between as required.

The list of defined locations appears at the top of Network Preferences. At first there'll only be one – Automatic – which is fine for regular DHCP-enabled networks. If you need to use others, select Edit Locations from the Locations drop-down. Click '+' to create a new entry and give it a name, such as Work or Home.

Choose the connection method, such as Ethernet, in the left-hand column, then choose the configuration method from the Configure IPv4 menu. If you're setting up your MacBook for a network without DHCP, choose Manually. Enter the required IP address, subnet mask and router addresses in the boxes below. If you don't know what these are, you should be able to obtain them from the network's sysadmin.

Click Apply to save your settings. You can switch between your location presets as required using the Location drop-down menu.

EXPRESS DELIVERY

If you regularly travel and need to use your MacBook and other devices with a variety of connections, pack an AirPort Express. This little gadget can be configured to convert an Ethernet connection to wifi or vice versa, and makes it easy to share one connection between devices.

Sharing and messaging

OS X makes it easy to set up your iCloud, email and social media accounts centrally, and offers apps for all kinds of communication.

Centralised accounts

The Mail, Contacts & Calendars pane of System Preferences handles social media too. Click a service in the right-hand column and you're invited to enter a valid username and password for it, which will then be used to access that service from the Share Sheets that OS X makes available in Finder windows, Safari, Contacts, Photo Booth and more.

The idea is that, for example, you can click to tweet a link or picture without having to log in to

← Share Sheets are available in several apps and the Finder, with an icon matching iOS' Share button.

Twitter. It's a good idea, but not yet fully implemented: try to share pictures to Flickr in iPhoto for the first time, say, and rather than accessing your central login, iPhoto will take you to a browser window to enter your details again.

As in iOS, OS X's built-in Twitter engine can add people's Twitter names to your Contacts and can stamp your tweets with a geographical position using Location Services, though you may prefer to decide whether to do this for each tweet.

If you need a service that isn't listed, pick Other to set up generic POP3 and IMAP email accounts, OS X Server user accounts, and other data services including LDAP, CardDAV and CalDAV.

↑ Mail, Contacts & Calendars also handles Twitter, Facebook, Yahoo!, Vimeo and Flickr, as well as services specific to users in East Asia.

← **iMessage can be glitchy, but it syncs chat across all your devices.**

Messages

Let's clear up one source of confusion first: Apple's instant messaging technology is called iMessage, but the app in which you use it is Messages. Replacing iChat, it also connects to AIM, Yahoo!, Google Talk and XMPP (also known as Jabber), so it's not only for talking to Apple users. But the Microsoft Notification Protocol, which would allow access to Windows Live Messenger, is absent. Nor does Microsoft offer a Messenger app; instead, Messenger IM is available from within the free Skype for Mac app.

You need to log in to Messages with a registered email address, allowing contacts to find you using details they already hold. You can register several email addresses with the app, but each will be tied to your Apple ID, and if you've not used an address before with Apple you'll need to verify it by clicking an emailed link.

Choose Preferences from the Messenger menu for a wide range of options for the app.

Once your accounts are set up, Messages is straightforward to use: just start typing the name of a contact and their details will pop up, or enter an IM handle, phone number or email address from scratch. It's superior to SMS in that instant messaging doesn't incur any network charges or eat up your text allowance, and messages can be received on your Mac as well as your phone.

Share Sheets (see opposite page) include a link to Message, so it's very quick and simple to message people pictures and links from the Finder, Safari and other Apple apps.

FaceTime

First seen in iOS, FaceTime is Apple's high-quality video chat service, and it's just as good on the Mac. The FaceTime HD camera built into the front of your MacBook is, as the name suggests, designed for the job, and you can either use the internal microphone, plug in the Apple EarPods that came with an iPhone (with their inline mic, which dangles closer to your mouth than your MacBook), add a third-party microphone headset or podcasting mic, or use a Bluetooth earpiece.

The catch with FaceTime is that it only works on Apple computers and devices. Note that you can also start a video chat in Messages with an AIM, Google Talk or Jabber buddy. Group chats are supported, but only within the same service.

↑ **FaceTime works between Macs and iOS.**

Mail

You'll probably spend quite a bit of your time in your email app, and OS X's Mail provides a capable and friendly environment.

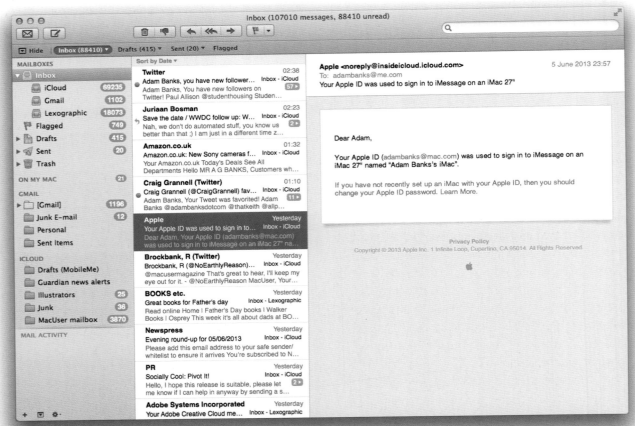

↑ **Apple's Mail app has an efficient layout and comprehensive email management features.**

It's not clear whether web-based email services such as Google Mail have become so popular because they're free, because browser access makes it easy to pick up your mail when away from your own computer, or just because people hate email software. Apple's Mail offers the best of all alternative: an iCloud account is indeed free, the Mail apps on both OS X and iOS are beautifully neat and usable, and if you prefer webmail you can log in via icloud.com and get your email that way.

Although the current version of Mail is still recognisably the app originally introduced as part of OS X 10.7 Lion in 2011, it's continued to evolve. Its collapsible interface makes good use of the space available whether you're on an 11in MacBook Air or a 27in iMac. Importantly for heavy users, the app is also happy with large quantities of mail, as you can see in the screenshot above.

→ You can set up your email accounts in Mail's Preferences, but it's now simpler to do it in the Mail, Contacts & Calendars pane of System Preferences.

The Mail app

A challenge for email apps is to present a lot of information without feeling cramped. It's only over time that you appreciate how cleverly Mail achieves this: the interface is strikingly light, with no chunky borders dividing its parts, yet the structure is clear. A modest amount of white space is intelligently used: the blue bullet that indicates an unread message sits in a narrow vertical strip that's otherwise unoccupied, making it unintrusive yet easy to scan.

Your mailboxes are listed to the left, with a unified Inbox at the top that displays all messages in all inboxes. Clicking Hide removes this column, devoting the whole of the window to your messages and the preview pane; resizing the window narrower has the same result. You can also adjust the width of each pane by dragging the vertical rules; make the list wide enough and the preview pane disappears. Double-clicking any message opens it in a separate resizeable window.

SORTING THE MAIL

In Preferences, you can create Rules to manage your mail. From the Mailbox menu, you can set up Smart Folders that always show all the messages meeting a certain set of criteria at any given time.

Conversations

When you receive a message that continues a thread with one or more other people, only that latest message appears in the email list, with a label at the right indicating how many emails are in the conversation; this can be clicked to list the others nested below. Click on the message itself and the preview to the right shows all the emails in the conversation in order.

This not only makes conversations easier to follow, but neatly groups recurring marketing and mailing list emails. Because senders usually quote the previous email when replying, you could end up with a lot of repetition in the conversation preview, but Mail is smart enough to avoid this by hiding the quoted sections, with a 'See more' link to reveal them. Inevitably, messages can end up in a conversation where they don't belong because they have a similar subject, or get omitted because they don't, but mostly conversations work well. If you disagree, you can turn off the feature in the View menu, or tweak it in Preferences > Viewing.

Reminders and more

OS X loves to remind you and alert you about things, which is pretty handy if you have too much going on to keep track of.

Calendar Previously iCal, the Calendar app may divide aesthetic opinion with its leather and torn-paper effects, but it's a smart time-tracking app. Besides storing appointments, it keeps an eye on reminders and due dates and lets you invite friends and colleagues to meetings.

Clicking the Calendars button at the left of the toolbar reveals whatever calendars have been set up, such as Work and Home. To add another, press Cmd-Alt-N and give it a name. You can show or hide calendars using their tick boxes. Each calendar is colour-coded, and these colours are replicated on any entries you create so you can see at a glance what they relate to.

A third default calendar – Birthdays – draws data from the Birthday field on contacts' entries in your address book. To use it, you'll need to opt in via Calendar > Preferences. It's on the front tab.

To have iCloud sync calendars between your Macs and iOS devices, tick Calendars & Reminders in the iCloud pane of System Preferences. You can also subscribe to other users' calendars over the internet (File > New Calendar Subscription) or make yours available to others (show calendars, then right-click one and choose Sharing Settings).

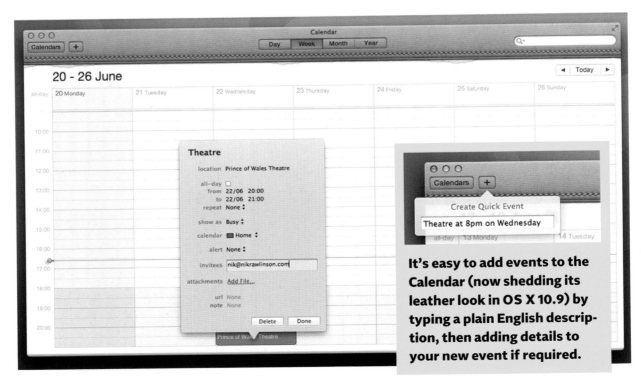

It's easy to add events to the Calendar (now shedding its leather look in OS X 10.9) by typing a plain English description, then adding details to your new event if required.

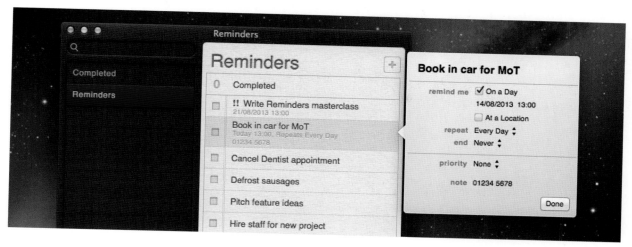

↑ Reminders is a simple task manager that makes it easy to keep yourself organised.

Calendar can work with other online calendars, such as Google's. To set this up, go to Calendar > Preferences and click Accounts. Click '+', select Google as the account type and enter your Google login details. The Calendar app will start to retrieve your existing appointments from Google's servers. Set how often you want it to refresh the local copy of your calendars: the default is every 15 minutes, which should be fine.

At this point, Calendar will only be reading changes from the server. So that it also writes back your changes, click Delegation and tick the boxes for the calendars you want to access.

Reminders

Just as the Notes app used to be part of Mail, Reminders has moved out of iCal as an app in its own right. Reminders is a simple to-do list maker rather than a fully fledged time manager in the Getting Things Done (GTD) mould, but it can handle priorities, deadlines and repeats, and lets you set reminders that pop up when a task is due.

A relatively new option is use your location to trigger an alert, so you can be reminded of something when you arrive at or leave somewhere. You'll need to enable Location Services in System Preferences > Security & Privacy > Privacy to get this working. Since your data will be synced via iCloud (assuming you opt for this), it won't matter if you've put down your MacBook and picked up your iPhone before making that move – it'll still know it's supposed to give you that reminder.

Notification Center

Clicking the icon at the far right of OS X's menu bar shifts the desktop to the left to reveal notifications, like sliding your finger down from the top of an iPhone. Sliding two fingers onto your MacBook's trackpad from the right does the same. Apps can send notifications to the Center; those that need immediate attention can also pop up a banner or a Growl-style alert. By default, each app gets to post its five most recent alerts to Notification Center, but you can increase or decrease this. All the settings are in Notifications in System Preferences.

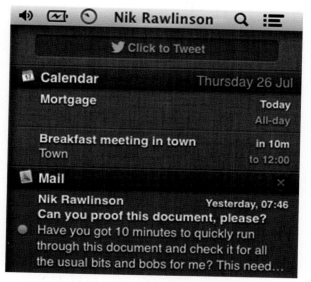

↑ Notifications let apps request attention.

Safari

OS X's web browser, based on the open source WebKit engine that Apple helped to create, is one of the Mac's essential apps.

Launched in 2003 to usurp Microsoft's Internet Explorer on the Mac, Safari is built on the WebKit rendering engine, also used on iOS devices. Some websites were slow to support Safari, but along with WebKit, which has become the nearest thing to an industry standard for browsers, it's now as widely accepted as the latest editions of Internet Explorer. It's installed as part of OS X, and its blue compass icon appears in the Dock by default.

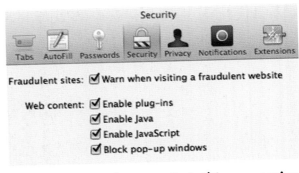

↑ Disabling Java (not JavaScript) is now a wise security move, unless you're sure you need it.

Switching browser If you prefer to use another browser, however, such as Google's Chrome (also based on WebKit), you're free to do so. Download and install it, then open Safari and go to Safari > Preferences. In the General tab, Default Web Browser will be set to Safari. Click this to drop down a list of alternatives, which should include your newly installed web browser; select it. If not, pick Choose and navigate to the browser in your Applications folder. Your browser will now be invoked wherever Safari usually would.

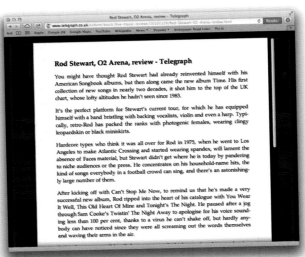

↑ When the Reader button turns blue, you can click it to reduce a cluttered web page to plain text.

↑ **Safari automatically fills its Top Sites display with live thumbnails of websites you often visit.**

Reader Some web pages today are so cluttered, it's hard to read the main text. Safari's Reader option looks for a large block of text on a page, pulls it out and displays it like a book page. Don't confuse with Reading List, which saves web pages for later.

iCloud tabs As long as you're signed in to iCloud in System Preferences and Safari is ticked, you can click this button to see which web pages are open in any tabs in Safari on other Macs or iOS devices (running Safari 6 or iOS 6 or higher) that are signed in with the same Apple ID, and they'll see yours.

Unified search Safari now has just one box at the top where you enter a web address or a phrase to search for – it'll figure out which is which, or you can choose from the menu that pops up.

Reading List | **iCloud tabs** | **Top Sites** | **Unified address/search bar** | **Reader** | **Downloads**

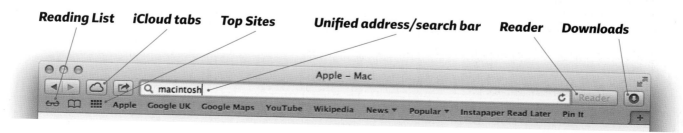

iTunes

Your gateway to the iTunes Store and the default place for all your entertainment on the Mac, the iTunes app keeps evolving...

A new look

With the arrival of iCloud, the iTunes app is no longer quite so central to Apple's OS X/iOS eco-system, but for many Mac users it's still the hub of their digital entertainment – not least because it incorporates the iTunes Store. Yet hardly anyone actually admits to *liking* it, which is why Apple has been working hard recently to improve it – with some pretty radical changes.

The redesign unveiled by Scott Forstall shortly before he was ousted from Apple really is different. Not only are there several new features, but familiar ones have been removed, including Cover Flow, the endlessly influential view where your albums flip past in a sort of horizontal stack, the central one becoming fully visible. (It's still found elsewhere in OS X, but we wonder for how long.) There's an interesting new way of browsing your albums, and the iTunes Store is better integrated and easier to find your way around.

Your library

The way your music is displayed has changed completely from earlier versions. Central to iTunes now is the new Album view, which presents covers in an endlessly scrolling grid. Like other OS X changes, this reflects what Apple obviously sees as a trend towards users swiping between full-screen apps in preference to opening multiple windows across the screen.

With Music selected in the drop-down menu at the top left of iTunes' main window, click Albums in the navigation bar just below the 'LCD'

display. You'll see all the albums in your Library arranged in a grid. By default, these include all the albums you've ever bought from the iTunes Store on the account that you're signed in as, whether or not they're present on your Mac now; and those you've added to this account from other sources using an iTunes Match subscription. iTunes Match is Apple's service that, for a small annual fee, lets you access all your music – whether bought from Apple or not – on all your Macs, PCs and iOS devices from the cloud.

↑ The new Mini Player, which can be used at the same time as iTunes' full view, lets you search for music and add tracks to Up Next without switching back to the main window. Roll over the window to reveal playback controls and an AirPlay icon, which also lets you adjust iTunes' volume on your remote wireless speakers.

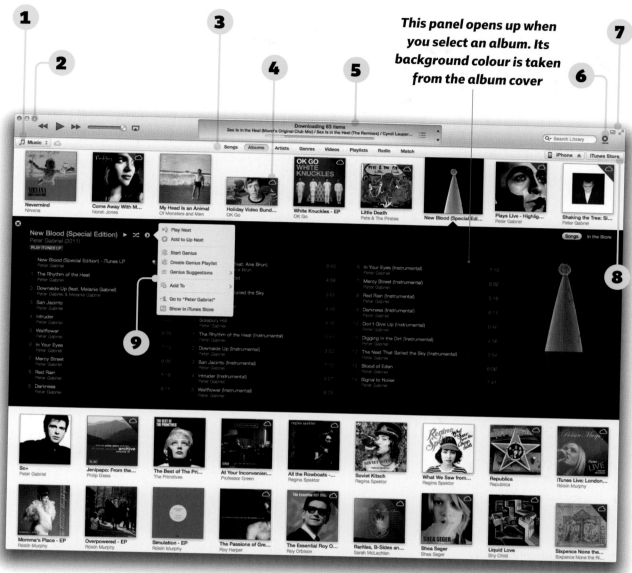

This panel opens up when you select an album. Its background colour is taken from the album cover

❶ Switch between your music, films, TV shows and other media, including audio CDs and shared iTunes libraries on your network, by clicking this pop-up.

❷ The green button now toggles the window between filling the desktop and going back to its *previous* size and position (not a preset).

❸ Each type of media can be viewed in several different ways. These options switch between the views available.

❹ Roll over the cloud at the top right of an item and it changes to a '+'. Click to download it. Or click elsewhere on an album cover for a track list, then use the cloud buttons beside tracks to download them.

❺ The 'LCD' display scrolls between statuses if several things are happening at once, like syncing an iPod while playing music. The large arrows at the right step through the various statuses manually.

❻ This icon shows the progress of iTunes Store downloads. Click it to monitor them in a separate window.

❼ The tiny icon on the left here switches iTunes to the Mini Player. The right one takes it into full-screen mode.

❽ This button takes you to the iTunes Store. It then changes to 'Library' to bring you back here.

❾ Click this circled arrow for actions related to the album or track.

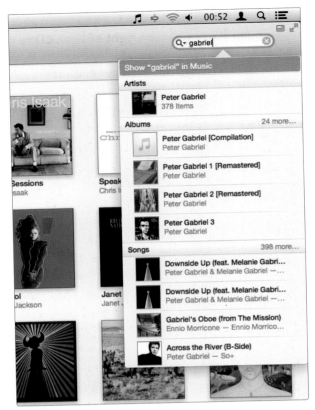

↑ You'll need to get the hang of the new search methods introduced in iTunes 11.

But which of the items you can see in iTunes are actually on your Mac ready to play, and which are a download away on Apple's servers? You can see which are in the cloud because a cloud icon appears at the top right of their covers. As you'd expect, clicking this gives you an option to download the item now.

Click on an album and the new expanded view slices into the grid. We've seen a similar effect when displaying groups of apps in iOS and in OS X's Launchpad, and Google has adopted a version of it in image search results, so it's obviously an idea whose time has come. It's a nice touch to colour the slice based on the colour of the album artwork, and iTunes does a good job of picking contrasting text colours that are readable on top of it. Tracks on the album are listed at the left, while a vignetted enlargement of the album artwork pretties things up at the right.

Click the Play button to the right of the title to play the album through, or the Shuffle icon to

mix it up. If you hover over one track, an arrow appears to the right of its name; click it to reveal a drop-down menu allowing you to add the track to a playlist, get Genius recommendations for others or find it in the iTunes Store. Note that Genius is turned off by default, so if you want iTunes to suggest new purchases that might be to your taste you'll need to enable it via Store > Turn On Genius.

Add your own music

Whatever you've bought on the iTunes Store will always appear in the iTunes app. To add music files that came to your Mac from elsewhere, you can drag a folder of tracks onto the iTunes icon in the Dock or select Add to Library (Cmd-O) from iTunes' File menu. MP3, AAC, Apple Lossless, AIFF and WAV formats are supported.

By default, anything you add is copied to the iTunes Media Library in the Music folder inside your home folder in Users. You can switch that to another folder, but it's important to allow iTunes to manage your music (and not to move it around manually) so that it can preserve playlists, artwork and so on. Your iTunes library can reside on a network storage device (NAS), but some users have reported problems using wifi storage for this.

If you need to change where iTunes stores your music, first copy your entire iTunes Media Folder to the new location (in the Finder). Then, in iTunes, go to Preferences > Advanced and ensure both the boxes below the file path display are ticked. Click Change, browse to your new iTunes Media Folder and Click Open.

Search in iTunes

The search box at the top right of iTunes' window works differently from iTunes 11 onward. When you start typing into it, a pop-up list of suggestions appears, much like with OS X's Spotlight menu. But if you type more than one keyword, the list only shows results in which all of those keywords appear in a single field. So if Björk's 'All is Full of Love' is in your Library, 'love full' would reveal it but 'bjork full of love' wouldn't. This seems a bit odd.

← Click the list icon at the right of the LCD to reveal Play Next and Up Next. These let you build ad-hoc playlists. Right-click any album or track and click Play Next to add it to the top of the list, so it plays after the current track; or choose Add to Up Next to append it to the bottom of the list. All tracks appear individually, even if added as an album. To remove a track, open the list and hover over an item to show a cross to its left. The arrow at its right lets you bump a track to the top; you can also drag items up and down the list to re-order.

The trick is to press Return in the box. The pop-up then disappears, and the content area of the main window filters to show items in which the keywords you type appear, in any combination of fields. You can type several keywords and then press Return, or press Return after the first to filter the search results as you type, progressively digging deeper into your library; press Space after Return to keep the keywords separate.

While still in the search box, press Esc to cancel the search and see all your content again, or click the cross to remove the search terms.

As in previous versions, the magnifying glass icon here pops up a list of fields so that you can explicitly restrict the search to, say, song title or artist. Above these options is a new one, Search Entire Library. Unticking this limits iTunes to searching the Library section you're currently in, disables the pop-up results behaviour, and reverts the search box to its classic mode of operation.

There's a search bar in the Mini Player as well, but at the time of writing this can't restrict searches, always displaying results from the entire library. When looking for multiple keywords it only shows results in which all of them appear in a single field, and ignores you hitting Return.

TV AND MOVIES

Besides music, the other types of media in your Library can also be viewed in several ways. Clicking a film's artwork shows a synopsis, cast and crew. Multiple series of a TV show are consolidated into a single item; click it and the expanded view has synopses of each episode and, at the top right, a series of buttons to flick between the various seasons. Special episodes are listed under No Season. There's also a new category, Home Videos, to distinguish your personal movies from bought films.

Image Capture

This surprisingly powerful little app is the key to getting photos and scanned images into your Mac with the least possible fuss.

Image Capture is one of OS X's underrated stars. Not only does it support scanners – extending that support to third-party apps – but it's also a more flexible way of downloading images from a camera than simply dragging them in the Finder.

Importing pictures

When you insert a camera's memory card in your Mac's card reader, connect a camera directly or plug in an iOS device, Image Capture may launch automatically. This behaviour is controlled from an options pane at the bottom left of Image Capture's window. Click the drop-down list and you can choose whether connecting this device in future will open Image Capture, Preview, iPhoto, some other app of your choice, or AutoImporter.

AutoImporter is an almost undocumented but very handy feature. To set it up, you first have to track it down. In the Finder, choose Go to Folder from the Go menu and type into the box: /System/Library/Image Capture/Support/Application. This will reveal the AutoImporter app. Double-click it, then go to the AutoImporter menu that appears next to the Apple menu and pick Preferences.

Here you can choose where images will be stored and set the name of a subfolder that will be created for each import. The blue labels for date, camera name, user name and sequence number can be dragged into the folder name box to add this metadata to the folder name.

It's safest not to tick 'Delete items from camera after successful import', because this

→ Click the tiny icon at the bottom left of Image Capture's window to set what happens when you attach a camera.

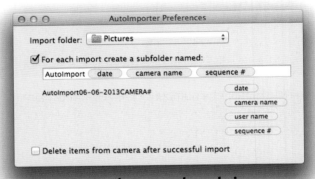

↑ AutoImporter is an even less obvious feature that further enhances Image Capture.

silently overrides the similar setting in Image Capture itself, which could catch you out if you forget you've set it up that way.

Once you've made these settings and closed AutoImporter, choose AutoImporter under 'Connecting this camera opens' in Image Capture. Next time you connect that device, all its images will automatically be copied to a new folder named in the way you specified. It may take a few tries to get the hang of it, but this can be a big time-saver.

Building a web page

Image Capture has a couple more surprises on its 'Import To' drop-down

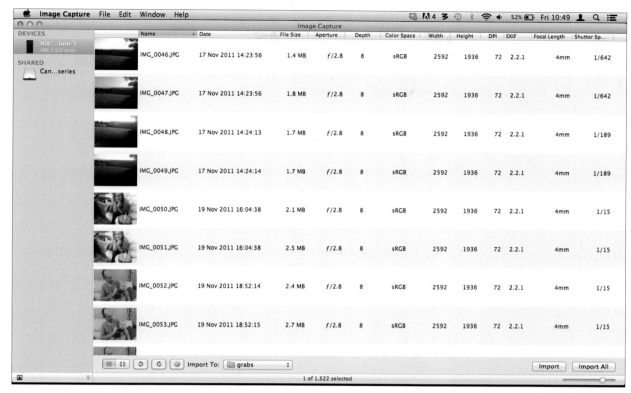

↑ Image Capture's list view shows both thumbnails and metadata, unlike the Finder.

↓ You can make a quick and dirty web page or PDF contact sheet directly on import.

menu. Highlight a number of images in the main view (first, select any that aren't the right way up and use the buttons below to rotate them), then pick Build Web Page from the 'Import To' menu and click Import at the far right. You don't even need to download your images – Image Capture will retrieve them from the storage medium as part of the process. The result is a very basic but handy web page showing all the images with their filenames for captions. Each thumbnail links to a larger version. The site is created in your Pictures folder, but you can drag it wherever you want it and edit the HTML using your preferred tools before uploading it to a web server.

Making an index PDF

Perhaps even more useful is the facility to create a PDF contact sheet of your selected images. Select some images, pick MakePDF from the 'Import To' menu and click Import to start. The MakePDF applet launches and shows your pictures laid

out on one or more pages; you can then use the Layout menu to adjust the size of the images, and MakePDF automatically reconfigures the layout, adding or removing pages as necessary. A range of standard image sizes is offered, with pictures either cropped or shrunk to fit, and you can also define and save your own custom sizes. Pick New Layout and choose a paper size (the default is Letter, so UK users will want to switch to A4) and image format. Opt to save your layout and you can use it again with future image imports.

Energy Saver

Apple's laptops have some of the longest-lasting batteries on the market, but wise configuration will get even more out of them.

How long your computer lasts before its battery needs recharging again will depend on a large number of factors, the most obvious being its battery capacity and age: batteries inevitably deteriorate as they get older, and eventually need replacing. These are factors largely beyond your control, though. What you *can* do is make sure you're not using any more electricity than necessary to do what you need to do.

An often heard piece of advice is to reduce the screen brightness to the lowest comfortable level, since the big, bright, high-resolution displays are one of the most power-hungry components of today's notebook computers. You can adjust the brightness using the F1 and F2 keys, which are marked for this function. (If this doesn't seem to work, try holding the Fn key while doing it. You can choose in System Preferences > Keyboard whether the F keys work as generic function keys with Fn and system control keys without, or vice versa.)

Mains vs battery

For more sophisticated tweaks, turn to the Energy Saver pane in System Preferences. The two tabs here let you set up different behaviours that vary the balance of performance and power consumption depending on whether your MacBook is running off its battery or the mains ('Power Adaptor'). Note that if you go to Energy Saver Preferences on a desktop Mac, you'll only see one set of options, but it's still worth reviewing the settings to minimise power consumption.

Each tab shows the same options. The two main sliders control how long your Mac should wait when not being used before blanking the display or putting itself to sleep. As you drag the marker along each scale, you'll see a live update of the exact time selected at the right-hand side.

Sooner or later?

It makes sense to set both of these features to kick in sooner when on battery than on mains power, but you might also want to bear in mind that the more frequently you make your machine sleep and wake up, the more (though only a tiny bit more) you'll stress its components. So the usual advice is to set a short display sleep time – say, two minutes – but delay full computer sleep to at least 15 minutes. You'll probably find it annoying if you set it lower than this in any case, since it's easy to get distracted for a few minutes in the middle of something – although MacBooks are quick to wake.

By default, OS X wants to put your Mac's hard disk to sleep whenever possible. If you have an actual hard disk, as in the MacBook Pro, rather than the solid state drives (SSD) used in MacBook Air and Retina MacBook Pro models, this will park its mechanical heads and cut the power. Again, that's not actually something you want to do more often than necessary, so it probably makes more sense to untick this option and forgo the marginal power saving. It's a good idea, on the other hand, to tick the box below, to slightly dim the display when on battery. Apple could have just let you set

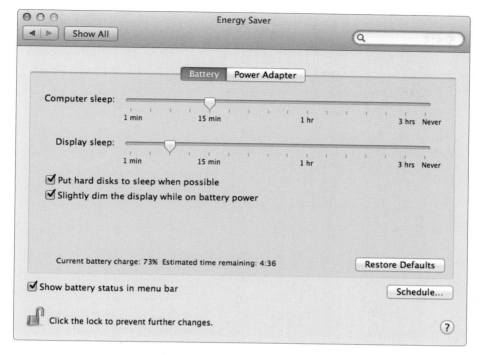

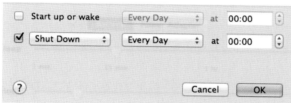

↑ You can set your Mac to act differently on battery power.

← Forgetting to shut down? Automate it!

day and don't want to sit around waiting for them to restart, then re-opening all our apps and documents.

In fact, MacUser has calculated that the energy saved by shutting an iMac down overnight, versus leaving it asleep, would be more than outweighed by the time the user would likely spend getting it ready for work again, using full power. The calculation is a bit different, though, when you're trying to avoid the battery going dead, not just save a few pence on electricity.

Fortunately, OS X now makes shutting down and starting up much less traumatic by automatically re-opening apps and windows, although you'll want to check that this actually works as expected with your favourite apps. So all things considered, you should think about shutting down your MacBook whenever you may not be using it for a while.

Energy Saver doesn't have an option to do this automatically after a period of inactivity, but what it can do is shut down your Mac every day (or some other time period) at a preset time – so if you're a creature of even a little bit of habit, you can probably pick a time when you won't be using it. Click the Schedule button at the bottom of the Energy Saver pane and tick the second box, setting the first option beside it to Shut Down. Choose the day or days to do this (named days, every day, weekdays or weekends) and a time.

If you want to be super-organised, you can even tell it to start up again before you start work the next day, to avoid having to wait for it.

a brightness level for each scenario, but this way is more convenient because if at any time you feel like tweaking the brightness, you can just do it (from the keyboard), knowing it'll still adjust itself from that point when you switch power source.

On the Power Adapter tab, the display brightness option is swapped for an option to wake on LAN access, which allows you to activate your MacBook remotely while it's asleep, if that's something you're likely to need to do.

Sleep vs shutdown

Even in sleep mode, your MacBook will continue to drain a trickle of power from its battery. Apple's own advice is that 'if you aren't going to use your MacBook Pro [or Air] for a couple of days or longer, it's best to shut it down'. But shutting down isn't a habit most Mac users have developed – after all, we use our Macs all hours of the

Windows on the Mac

Your MacBook can run Windows if you need it to, just the same as a PC. But what's the best way to install it – native or virtualised?

Compatibility   Time and again, the MacBook range is ranked among the world's best-selling computer brands, while the machines themselves are rated the best quality. So why would anyone *not* choose an Apple laptop? One odd reason is the perception that they can't run Windows. Of course, with most software categories thoroughly covered by OS X apps, the typical Mac user is more than happy not to have to use Microsoft's operating system.

Still, some of us do need to run a Windows app now and again, whether for a specialist hobby or compatibility with legacy systems at work. And what's often overlooked is that every Mac is quite capable of running Windows. It's just not the operating system that happens to come with it.

True, there are a couple of fiddly bits of setup that you wouldn't have with a PC, and buying your own copy of Windows is annoyingly expensive. On the plus side, though, you won't be stuck with all the unwanted promotional apps that PC makers shovel into their Windows installations. That's a serious advantage: when IT support company Soluto calculated in May 2013 which laptops gave the best Windows performance, it put an Apple MacBook at the top of the table, ahead of the likes of Acer and Dell, and admitted part of the reason was that its Windows installation was 'clean'.

In the past, when Macs and PCs each used different types of processor chips, running Windows required emulation, which tended to compromise performance. Now that Macs use the same Intel chips as PCs (for the moment, at least – both could move in other directions) there are no such concerns. So the Mac trumps the PC, being the only platform on which you can run all three common operating systems – Windows, OS X and variants of Unix – and have access to the widest possible range of software.

Corporate users should no longer be told their IT systems can't support Macs, since by adding Windows they can run apps that aren't available for OS X and access services that depend on Windows-only client software from the likes of Microsoft. In fact, by standardising on Macs, businesses of all sizes can put the same machine on every desk, whatever software each user might need or prefer, which could simplify support and save money. Gamers can install Windows titles without waiting for the Mac version to appear.

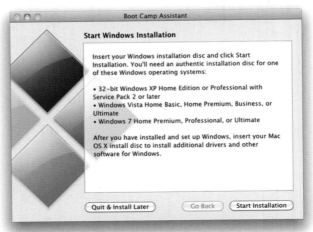

↑ Boot Camp tools are provided by Apple to help you install Windows on your Mac.

↑ It's kind of freaky, but since Macs and PCs use the same basic types of hardware, Windows will run directly on a MacBook. You only need extra trickery if you want to integrate it with OS X.

Every Mac comes with Apple's Boot Camp utility to help you get Windows set up, so all you need to add is a full copy of Windows. With this installed, you can choose whether your Mac is a Mac or a PC each time you start it up.

Before you wade in and begin the installation, though, it's worth considering 'virtualisation' products that let you run Windows apps and OS X apps at the same time, on the same screen. This magical capability saves you switching between operating systems, and you'll still get maximum performance from each OS. The leading contenders are Parallels Desktop and VMware Fusion, and we'll take a close look at both in a moment.

How to buy Windows

You'd think if a user of the rival Apple platform wanted to pay Microsoft money for Windows, Microsoft would be pretty happy about it. But

apparently not, because in releasing the latest version of its OS, Windows 8, Microsoft has stopped selling full boxed copies: all the Windows 8 packages you see advertised are upgrades, requiring an existing Windows installation. Most copies of Windows 8 come pre-installed on new PCs. If you do already have an earlier version of Windows on your Mac (Windows XP SP3, Vista or Windows 7), you can upgrade it, and that includes the Windows 8 Consumer Preview and Release Preview beta versions that were available free of charge for a while before Windows 8's launch.

Microsoft has confirmed the only way for a consumer to install Windows 8 fresh on a clean system, such as a new Mac, is to buy an 'OEM System Builder' edition – the brown box package intended to be used by smaller PC vendors to install Windows on the systems they sell. This comes with no technical support (although your statutory rights as a consumer still apply) and is

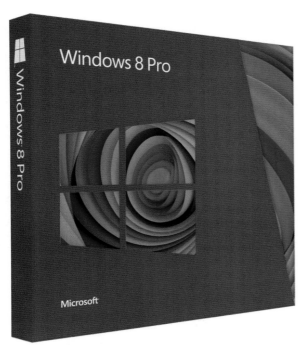

↑ This pretty box is no use to you – it'll only work on a system already running Windows.

only licensed for one machine – you can't transfer your copy of Windows to a different Mac later.

As long as you can live with those limitations, Windows 8 OEM is widely available from outlets such as Amazon. We found it at £69.99 inc VAT in the UK or $89.99 in the US; the Pro version was selling for £104.99, or US$130.55.

The standard edition will be fine for most users, but if you need more extensive encryption (perhaps because you're handling sensitive data), the ability to access your PC remotely using Remote Desktop Connection, or the option to connect to a corporate or school network that uses Windows Server Domains and Group Policies, you'll need to pay extra for Pro. If you don't, however, and change your mind later, upgrading to Pro is a simple matter of entering a new serial number to unlock features. You can buy the necessary code by searching online stores for 'Windows 8 Standard Edition to Windows 8 Pro Pack'.

Microsoft also offers cut-down versions called Windows 8 N and Windows 8 Pro N. These lack the full edition's media playback features, so if you buy them you'll have to find your own apps for playing music and DVDs. Microsoft was forced to sell these editions in an EU anti-monopoly settlement, and they're generally ignored.

Many MacBooks have no DVD drive, so you may need to buy a download version of Windows rather than physical media. You'll then need to copy the downloaded ISO file to an external USB stick of 8GB or higher capacity. Even if you use a Windows DVD in a Mac with a SuperDrive, let Boot Camp Assistant create a flash memory-based installer as part of the setup process – it's a standard option on the second screen of the installer. If you've also opted to download the latest Windows support software, it'll copy this to the same USB stick so it's ready for use during the setup process.

Even if you don't want to copy the installation media to a USB drive, perhaps because you don't have one big enough handy, you'll still need to download the drivers and install them via USB. For Windows 8 you'll need the Boot Camp 5 Support Software, which you can download from support.apple.com/kb/DL1638. Extract the compressed zip file and copy the $WinPEDriver$ folder to a FAT-formatted USB drive. You can format the USB drive as FAT (which is standard for Windows disks, not for Mac) using Disk Utility, which you'll find on your Mac in the Utilities folder in Applications, along with Boot Camp Assistant.

WHEN I'M 64-BIT

You'll find both 32-bit and 64-bit versions of Windows advertised. Outwardly they work just the same, but there are important differences in their ability to access memory and processor cores. Version 5 of the Boot Camp Support Software, which is required for Windows 8 and supplied with OS X Lion and Mountain Lion, will only run 64-bit Windows. If you have an older Mac with Boot Camp 4 Software Support and are thinking of installing Windows 7, you can choose 32-bit or 64-bit; the latter may deliver marginal performance improvements at the expense of incompatibility with a few old apps or drivers.

Installing Windows with Boot Camp

Boot Camp will run on any recent Mac. To use it to install Windows, you'll also need 2GB of RAM; 20GB of free hard drive space to install Windows 7 for the first time, or 30GB for Windows 8, or 40GB if you're upgrading from a previous version; a Windows installation DVD or disk image file in ISO format and a FAT-formatted USB drive onto which you can download the necessary Windows drivers (see above). You can't install Windows onto an external

THE LATEST THING

Windows 8 is compatible with these Macs:

MacBook Air (Mid 2011 or newer)
MacBook Pro (15/17in, Mid 2010 or newer)
MacBook Pro (Early 2011 or newer)
iMac (27in, Mid 2010 or newer)
iMac (21.5in, Mid 2011 or newer)
Mac mini (Mid 2011 or newer)
Mac Pro (Early 2009 or newer)

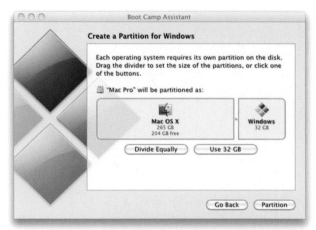

↑ **Partitioning your MacBook's hard drive is the first step towards installing Windows.**

drive using Boot Camp, so if your MacBook's short of space you'll need to clear it out or look at Parallels or VMware, which let you run Windows on an external drive. Nor does Boot Camp support Windows on a RAID or Software RAID setup.

With your shiny new copy of Windows at the ready, prepare your Mac using Boot Camp Assistant. You'll find this in the Utilities folder inside Applications (or just search for it using Spotlight). It's been installed with every version of OS X from 10.5 Leopard onwards. Boot Camp Assistant performs several functions in sequence, the most important of which is to split your hard drive into two uneven sections, one of which will continue as before while the new, usually smaller portion is reserved solely for Windows' use.

It's important to ensure all of the drivers on your Mac have been updated to the latest

versions available before you begin, so use the Software Update feature on the Apple menu to check for recently posted updates. Then make sure you have a full backup of your system. If you've been using Time Machine, you have, but consider making a separate backup too, perhaps using a disk cloning utility such as SuperDuper! or Carbon Copy Cloner. Having said that, it would be unusual for the installation to go horribly wrong. But do plug your MacBook into the mains, because running out of battery at a critical point while repartitioning the drive could be awkward.

With your system updated and backed up, open Boot Camp Assistant and walk through the setup screens. It's all fairly self-explanatory, and if you're uncertain, Apple provides a set of simple instructions for download at manuals.info.apple.com/en_US/boot_camp_install-setup_10.8.pdf with plenty of troubleshooting tips. It's well worth downloading and printing out this document before you start, just in case you can't later.

Make sure that when Boot Camp offers to create a partition for your new operating system, you set it to a minimum of 30GB, assuming you're installing Windows 8. You should give it considerably more space than this if you have room on your drive and expect to install a fair amount of Windows software, since each app will have to fit alongside Windows in this dedicated partition. Unlike Parallels Desktop and VMware Fusion, Boot Camp won't dynamically increase the size of your Windows drive when it starts to get full, so try to err on the generous side at the start.

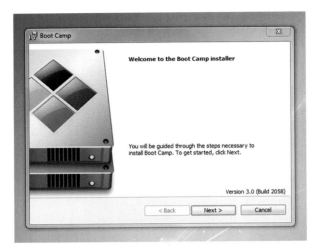

↑ Only halfway through the process, and your MacBook is already running Windows!

Your Mac will reboot during the installation process so that it can run the native Windows installer within its own environment rather than under OS X. Once this is complete, it'll go on to install the specific drivers required to access the hardware on your Mac, including wifi, the integrated camera, keyboard, mouse and so on.

Boot Camp should install these drivers automatically, but if it doesn't you can install them manually by opening the Boot Camp folder on the USB drive you made earlier and dou-ble-clicking setup.exe from inside the Windows

NETWORK NEWS

Even when you're running Windows, a Boot Camp installation (and the same goes for the virtual machines we'll cover next) uses your Mac's existing network connections – whether wired or wireless – to connect to the internet. This saves you having to fiddle with Windows' own network settings to get online, and an extra benefit is that Boot Camp (or your virtualisation solution) can keep an eye out for any updates and patches that it needs to download, either for Windows itself or any installed security apps, and can deal with these in the background.

environment. Windows may bring up a warning that the software hasn't passed Windows Logo testing; just click Continue Anyway to complete the process.

Choosing which OS to use

With Windows installed via Boot Camp, your Mac can run OS X or Windows, but not both at once. So you have to choose which operating system to load at the point of booting up your Mac. Assuming you use one OS more than the other, it'll save you time to set the default option that the machine will go with on startup unless you interrupt it to say otherwise.

↑ Hold Alt as you restart to choose which OS to load, or preset this in System Preferences.

To do this, start up in Windows, and if you're using Windows 7 pick Boot Camp Control Panel from the system tray (at the bottom right of the screen); or in Windows 8, search for Boot Camp, then click Settings and Boot Camp. Here, pick the OS you want to load on startup by default. Then, in OS X, go to System Preferences, click Startup Disk and again select your preferred OS.

But if you've just set up Boot Camp and you'll only be running Windows occasionally, just leave OS X as the default system. When you do want to start up in Windows, hold Alt from the start of the boot process until your Mac brings up the drive selection menu. Pick Windows. To return to OS X next time, either reboot and use the same method to choose OS X, or click the Boot Camp icon in the Windows system tray and click 'Restart in OS X'.

IS IT SAFE?

Mac users don't usually have to think much about security beyond installing occasional Software Updates. Few of us run anti-virus software, because Mac viruses are extremely rare. Although social engineering or 'phishing' attacks, such as enticing people to install malicious software or type their bank details into fake websites, can affect Mac users just like anyone else, there's relatively little reason to worry about more insidious threats in OS X. But installing Windows means your Mac faces the same risks as any PC. The fact that Windows exhibits a wider range of security vulnerabilities is well publicised, and inviting it onto your Mac invites them too. Windows-specific attacks can strike your Windows installation, and if you've opted to share OS X folders with Windows, they could be corrupted, for example, by malware.

So you may want to install Windows anti-virus software. Parallels Desktop comes with trial subscriptions to security suites from Kaspersky and Norton, which will keep watch for viruses and Trojans, spyware, adware, rootkits and more. After the trial expires, you can pay a fee for continued protection. VMware Fusion includes a complimentary 12-month subscription to McAfee Anti-Virus Plus. Boot Camp comes without any third-party security tools. If you want to add your own, the three options already mentioned can be bought separately, among others. Windows 8 comes with a beefed-up version of Windows Defender that claims to provide the same protection as the free Microsoft Security Essentials did in Windows 7, but you may feel it's worth adding one of the above products or another security suite for extra protection. Do install all Windows updates.

Other ways to run Windows apps free

Before we move on to paid-for options, there are a couple of other ways you can get Windows apps running on your Mac for free. VirtualBox is free to download from virtualbox.org; originally developed by Sun Microsystems, it now belongs to Oracle, and offers many of the same features as VMware Fusion and Parallels Desktop, including Seamless Mode, which lets you run Windows apps without the surrounding Windows interface.

You can share OS X folders with Windows, either as read-only or with full access. They're seen as network shares, rather than integrated into the local file system, but can be set to auto-mount, so they're given their own drive letter in Windows.

VirtualBox doesn't work as smoothly as its paid-for rivals. In MacUser's tests, it didn't install its add-on utilities by default, so we had to manually add them later to get all of its features, including Seamless mode. And it couldn't determine our screen resolution, refusing to render any aspect ratio other than 4:3 until we'd gone into and out of full-screen mode twice. It didn't make any of the existing virtual machines on our test Mac available for conversion, or spot our Boot Camp partition. But installing Windows from disc caused no problems, and the process was identical to the non-'express' methods for Parallels and Fusion. Remember you still need to pay for Windows.

CrossOver Mac is completely different. It doesn't run Windows at all, but uses the Wine ('Windows emulator') compatibility layer to provide the hooks that Windows apps need to run *without* Windows, using OS X's Unix underpinnings. It's faceless except for a small utility via which you install the Windows apps you want.

The number of apps supported is growing all the time, with most of the business essentials covered, but check the apps you need at codeweavers.com/compatibility to make sure they'll work. You'll also need the installation disc or a disk image for each app to install it. But CrossOver will download free apps, such as Internet Explorer, mIRC or Word Viewer 2007, as part of its own installation process.

If the app you need isn't yet supported, you can propose it via CodeWeavers' website, and when enough votes are cast it may get added.

CrossOver also lets you choose the version of Windows you want to emulate, subject to compatibility, with each app. Because apps actually run within the X11 environment on top of the Unix core of OS X, they may not look as good in CrossOver Mac as they do in Windows itself.

Windows hypervisors

If you're planning to install Windows on a Mac, it's probably to run a specific app or two, or to test projects such as websites on the PC. The rest of the time you'll be running Mac software under OS X. Switching over every time you need to do a quick job in Windows will be a pain, and having apps for each system in a separate environment makes it a hassle to move information between them. So it's probably worth paying more for a product that lets Windows and OS X run side by side.

Such utilities create a series of 'virtual machines' running on your Mac's physical hardware, each being an installation of an operating system. You can even have apps running in other OSes inside windows on the OS X desktop. This is made

ACTIVATE OR WAIT?

Unlike OS X, each installation of Windows must be 'activated'. This ties it to the setup on which it's installed. If you plan to try several virtualisation products before settling on one, make sure you untick the option to activate Windows that appears when you enter the product licence key. You'll then be given 30 days' grace before you have to activate, enough for you to decide before committing your Windows licence to one installation.

possible by an extra software layer on top of OS X, known as a hosted hypervisor, which passes the demands of the guest operating system – Windows, Linux or something else – to your Mac's hardware, which does all the leg work and then passes back the results. This happens in real time, and with a modern Mac you can expect Windows performance similar to an equivalent PC.

The two leading hypervisor apps on the Mac are Parallels Desktop and VMware Fusion. Let's take a look at their latest versions (at the time of writing) in turn.

NO TIME FOR BACKUPS

Virtual machines are a problem for Time Machine, OS X's backup facility. Each is contained in a single huge file. Every hour you use it, this file will have changed, so Time Machine will back it up – quickly eating your backup space. Instead, add your virtual machine(s) to the Ignore tab in Time Machine Preferences, and back them up periodically by other means. Fusion, Parallels Desktop and VirtualBox can create snapshots of your machine as it stands at a given time, so you can roll back to a 'good' snapshot if anything bad happens. Boot Camp doesn't work this way, so Time Machine is fine with it.

VMware Fusion 5

VMware Fusion 5 is optimised for OS X 10.8 Mountain Lion and Windows 8. It supports USB 3 and Retina display, and compared to earlier versions VMware says it's faster and offers enhanced battery management.

We installed the 64-bit version of Windows 8 (see p68) under OS X 10.8 on a MacBook Pro with a 2.4GHz Intel Core 2 Duo processor and 4GB of RAM – a fairly modest specification. Setup was easy and took just under half an hour, including creating a Windows account. You can opt for the express method, which chooses the most common settings and activates the OS (but see 'Activate or wait?', above), or step through the custom installation, as we did. Fusion allocated the virtual machine containing our Windows installation one processor core and 1GB of memory.

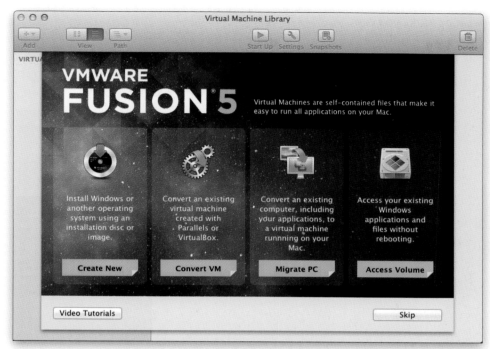

← **VMware's installer makes the process as simple as possible, and gives you the option to convert a Boot Camp, Parallels or VirtualBox installation of Windows, or even migrate an existing PC to a virtual machine on your Mac, usually via a USB hard drive.**

Booting Windows 8 for the second time, after the system had been optimised, took 47 seconds. Resuming a suspended machine took 35 seconds.

OS X's multi-touch scrolling transfers smoothly to Windows, and tile-based apps using what Microsoft used to call the Metro interface run well in full-screen. Windows 8's Charms, tools for tasks like search and sharing that slide in as you move the mouse to the right-hand side of the screen, work fine when you're running Windows full-screen or in a single window, but they don't work in Unity mode, which lets you run individual Windows apps on the OS X desktop. And we couldn't activate OS X's Dictation in Windows.

In OS X's Mission Control, Fusion accurately renders your Windows virtual machine on its own desktop, and it does the same with Metro-style apps; but you can't give over the whole screen in this way to a standalone Windows 7-style app. If you run a single Windows app more than once at the same time (impossible with most OS X apps, but normal for Windows), Mission Control renders all its instances in the same way it would group the multiple windows of a single instance of an OS X app. OS X Notifications are also well integrated.

VMware throws in 18 months of complimentary email support, and for new users there's also a year's subscription to McAfee Anti-Virus Plus, although you have to pay for it after that. Alternatively, you could rely on Windows 8's enhanced Windows Defender, or install the free Microsoft Security Essentials for earlier versions.

Other features include support for 3D in Linux, better handling of SSDs for faster boot and resume, and compatibility with a wider range of guest operating systems, including the option to run more of them at once. Up to 8GB of RAM can be allocated to each virtual machine, and the overall memory headroom has been raised to 60GB.

Fusion 5 also has a Professional version, which adds support for restricted virtual machine containers that limit what end users can do and allow sysadmins to disable features like connecting USB devices. Virtual machines in this business-oriented version can be encrypted and deployed en masse using a standard configuration, and you also get access to bundled support.

Parallels Desktop 8

Installing 64-bit Windows 8 under Parallels Desktop 8 took just under half an hour, the same as with VMware Fusion 5, using the same hardware. Like Fusion, Parallels assigned our virtual machine one CPU

↑ Parallels is a little more expensive than Fusion, but the integration of Windows is even tighter.

core and 1GB of memory. You can either use the custom option, for full control over the installation process, or opt for express if you're happy with the most common settings. If you're already running Windows using Boot Camp, you can import your virtual machine from there. Cold-booting Windows 8 for the second time took one minute and three seconds, while resuming from a suspended state took 43 seconds – both slower than Fusion 5's times, but reasonable.

Parallels' integration with OS X is even better than Fusion 5's. Beyond gesture controls and Notification Center access, it extends OS X's Dictation tool to Windows apps. Sharing OS X folders with Windows is no problem, as in earlier versions, but another advantage over Fusion is that it's now easier to share files between the two OSes simply by dragging them between windows containing the two environments.

Multiple instances of the same Windows app are gathered together in Mission Control, and unlike Fusion, Parallels also shows full-screen Windows apps correctly as separate desktops. But

again, Windows 8's handy Charms don't appear when you're using Coherence mode, Parallels' way of seamlessly mixing virtualised and OS X applications without the surrounding Windows or Linux interface. Still, they're easier to call up than with Fusion when you're running Windows in a single window, because a new 'sticky' window edge briefly clings to your mouse pointer as you hit it, rather than letting you slip straight out into OS X.

Right-clicking a Windows app in the Dock calls up the usual contextual menu, which gains an Add to Launchpad option. This works with tiles as well as full apps, so if you prefer Windows' weather app to the OS X Dashboard's Widget, for example, Launchpad can help you find it quickly.

A new Presentation Wizard disables screen-savers in both Windows and OS X simultaneously and shuts down any incoming Notifications so that you won't be interrupted in front of your audience if you're presenting from Windows.

Parallels also adds a new button to the Safari toolbar in OS X that opens your current page in Internet Explorer for Windows. It's unlikely you'll need to use this nowadays to open pages in IE that don't work in Safari – IE 10 and Safari 6 both score the full 100 in the Acid3 CSS test, and come very close in the HTML5 compliance tests at html5test.com – but it could be handy occasionally.

Parallels Desktop 8 feels more tightly integrated with OS X than Fusion 5. It's easier to share files between the native and virtual environments, and simple touches like the ability to run the tiled environment in Windows smaller than 1024 × 768 (Microsoft's stated minimum), which Fusion couldn't do in our tests, make it more flexible.

Parallels Mobile

Parallels Mobile lets you run Windows, Linux or OS X on an iPad or iPhone. Of course, that's impossible – the trick is that it connects remotely to your Mac, which needs to be running a Windows or Linux guest OS in Parallels Desktop 6 or later, or OS X in version 7 or later. It's easy to set up, with a dedicated Mobile pane in Parallels Desktop's Preferences that ties it to an account on Parallels' servers. Using the same login details in the Parallels Mobile app on the iPad or iPhone links it up over any internet connection, or you can use a local IP address to stream it over your internal network.

Some simple but smart multi-touch gestures get around the lack of a keyboard and mouse. Tapping three fingers calls up a menu overlay from which you can shut down, suspend or pause, open the keyboard and settings, or draw a marquee to select multiple objects or lines of text. Other gestures are a hybrid of conventional iOS actions and traditional trackpad motions.

KEYBOARD CONUNDRUM

Mac and Windows keyboards have several differences. Windows' Start key is absent from Macs, while the Cmd key, exclusive to the Mac, serves purposes handled by the Alt and Ctrl keys in Windows. Virtualisation products do a certain amount of translation, and you can trigger tasks like capturing screen grabs, for which you'd normally use key shortcuts, from the parent application's menus. But Boot Camp users may find it's worth investing in a Windows keyboard for bespoke buttons, such as PrntScrn (which copies the contents of your display), that don't have direct Mac equivalents.

Running Windows at 2048 × 1536, to match our Retina iPad, we could read on-screen text clearly even though it was small, and windows moved around smoothly. You can even (with Parallels Desktop 7 or later) copy and paste data between iOS and remote apps. It's a useful option.

⬇ Parallels Mobile gives you Windows on an iPad, courtesy of your Mac.

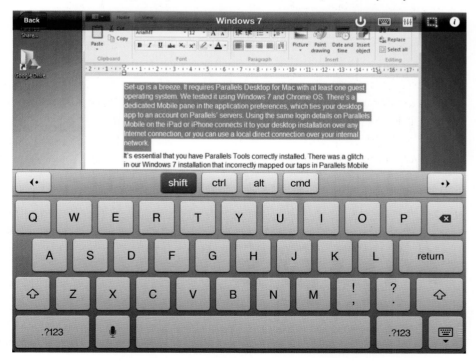

Chapter 3
Apps

Installing apps

Whether you buy them from the Mac App Store, in a box or from software makers' own websites, it's easy to add apps to your Mac.

The Mac App Store
When Apple launched the App Store for iPhone in 2008, it was a breakthrough, because it hadn't previously been possible for independent developers to make programs for that device. Of course, it's been possible to buy third-party software for Macs ever since the first Mac appeared in 1984, so the Mac App Store, introduced in January 2011, isn't so earth-shattering. But it's still useful in several ways.

Accessed from a circular Dock icon labelled with the 'A'-like symbol for applications, the App Store provides a single place for any Mac software maker to offer their apps to every user. All you need to access the Store, as with the iTunes Store, is an Apple ID: an account set up at appleid.apple.com (or in iTunes, or while setting up your Mac) that's tied to an email address – your free Apple me.com or icloud.com address, or an existing email, such as a Gmail account – and a password.

You'll normally attach a credit or debit card to your Apple ID when you set it up, and any purchases you make while logged in will be charged to this without you having to enter the details again.

Allow applications downloaded from:
○ Mac App Store
○ Mac App Store and identified developers
◉ Anywhere

↑ **Gatekeeper is a feature that optionally limits which apps can be installed on a Mac.**

Already, the simplicity of this approach has led to a fall in software prices, with Apple itself leading the way. Even its advanced professional products, such as Final Cut Pro X, are surprisingly affordable, while the popular iWork office apps – Pages, Numbers and Keynote – are available from the App Store at pocket-money prices.

All App Store apps, whether made by Apple or not, have been vetted by Apple, so you know they don't contain viruses or any other malware and are of decent quality. You're licensed to install them on all the Macs you own, not just one, and to facilitate this the App Store's Purchases tab lists all the apps attached to your Apple ID, so you can download them again as necessary. The Updates tab (which is where the Software Update item on the Apple menu also brings you) lists available updates to any installed apps and to OS X itself; the updates listed here are always free, and you just have to click Update or Update All to apply them.

Gatekeeper
One of the features that makes OS X relatively safe from malicious software is its robust control over application permissions, which means no executable code – that is, programs capable of running, as opposed to passive data files – can be installed or run on your Mac until you've explicitly approved that action. Now Gatekeeper adds an extra layer of security.

Gatekeeper checks any new software that tries to install itself to find out whether it's been approved by Apple via the Mac App Store; signed

↑ The Mac App Store is the obvious place to find new software to install, but not the only one.

off by an identified third-party developer through Apple's registration scheme (the programming code in the app is linked to the Developer ID, so Gatekeeper will know if the code has been tampered with); or neither of the above.

By default, the last category, the riskiest, isn't permitted, so if you get hold of an app of some sort from around the internet and try to install it, you'll be told you can't. But sometimes you may want to, when you're quite happy that you know where the app is from and trust its source. If so,

DISC WORLD

Some apps are still sold on discs rather than as downloads. If your MacBook has no DVD drive, you can add Apple's external SuperDrive, which is reasonably priced and plugs in via USB, to access these.

go to System Preferences, click Security & Privacy, pick the General tab, and change the option 'Allow applications downloaded from:' to 'Anywhere'. You'll be warned one last time that this is insecure; click Allow From Anywhere to confirm, and you can install whatever code you like, although you'll be asked for your Admin password each time.

If you prefer more security rather than less, you can set the option to 'Mac App Store', meaning only apps that are downloaded through the App Store can be installed and run. At the moment, Apple imposes some technical restrictions on App Store apps, as well as taking a 30% cut of their selling price, so while many major apps are sold through the App Store – including all of Apple's own – many others aren't. The ability to edit Gatekeeper's options means that, unlike iOS, OS X isn't limited to running apps that Apple has vetted, but if you do want the security of that kind of 'walled garden', you can simply switch it on.

Preview and TextEdit

TextEdit provides basic word processing, while the highly capable Preview app can display many document formats and edit PDFs.

Available in the Dock by default, the **Preview** app's icon represents a desk magnifier, and it's your first choice for looking at most kinds of documents. With iCloud becoming a more important part of OS X, it's a particularly handy way to access files you've stored in the cloud. Click its Dock icon to open Preview, and press Cmd-O for Open.

The iCloud tab shows files you've stored in your iCloud space from other Mac apps or on your iPhone or iPad (if Preview is able to read their file format). You can even drag a new file onto this tab from the Finder to put it in the cloud, and it'll be synced with other Macs logged in to the same iCloud account. However, at the time of writing, files you add this way don't appear on iOS devices.

Editing PDFs

Preview supports 28 file types, including some you might not expect, such as Adobe Illustrator and Microsoft PowerPoint. An important one is PDF (Portable Document Format), which is widely used to exchange all kinds of documents while preserving their appearance, including work documents you might be sent for approval and forms you need to fill in. You could use the free Adobe Reader app to open these, but Preview is fully equipped for the job.

When you open a PDF in Preview, the first page appears in the main part of the window and a thumbnail list of all the pages appears in a sidebar. Press Cmd-Alt-2 to open this if you don't see it, or click the leftmost button in the toolbar at the top to drop down a menu of options. You can

LIKE A VERSION

Preview and TextEdit are among the few apps that make full use of OS X's Versions (see p43), which means saving works differently. In other apps, if you want to save a new copy of the file you're working on, in its current state, you press Cmd-Shift-S for Save As, and enter a new name; you're now working on this new file. But when you use the same shortcut in Preview or TextEdit, the original file stays open independently, while an identical copy is created in a new window. This isn't saved until you press Cmd-S and name it. Keep in mind that the original document is still sitting open: if you later save it, any changes you'd made *before* using Cmd-Shift-S will be applied. If you find this confusing, the good news is you can still access the traditional Save As command: just hold the Alt key, either while clicking the File menu or while pressing Cmd-Shift-S. The new file handling system does have its benefits. For example, if you forget to save a file at all, and quit Preview or TextEdit or even shut down your Mac, when you go back to that app your work will still be there.

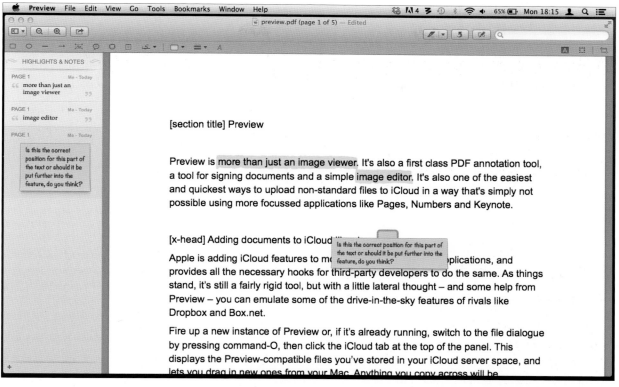

↑ **Preview is much more than just a document viewer: it also lets you re-order, annotate and sign PDFs; edit, resize and crop images; and export a variety of documents in different formats.**

remove a page by selecting it and pressing Cmd-Backspace, or change the page order simply by dragging pages up and down in the sidebar. With longer documents, it may help to switch to the Contact Sheet view by pressing Cmd-Alt-5 (again, you can choose this from the menu).

Preview's annotation tools also let you add notes and call-outs to PDF pages, ready to send back to other users, instead of printing the document and scribbling in the margins. To highlight a word or phrase, drag across it and click the highlighter button in the toolbar. The default colour

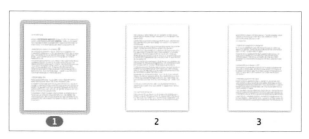

↑ **Re-order PDF pages by dragging them in Preview's Thumbnail or Contact Sheet views.**

is yellow, but you can change it by clicking the downward arrow beside the button. Notice that the line is slightly wavy, as if applied by hand. On the same menu are underline and strikethrough.

To go further, click Show Edit Toolbar – the last button on the right, beside the search box. If you want to draw a circle around a section of text, for example, either select the text and then click the oval tool, or click the tool with no text highlighted and then drag out an oval to size.

Other tools, such as the text box and speech bubbles, add text on top of the document. But the note tool is the most useful, letting you place small 'sticky notes' anywhere on the page, linked to selected text, so you needn't cover up the text.

Preview indexes your annotations, so you (or someone you've sent the document to) can view all your notes and changes in a sidebar and skip between them, using Cmd-Alt-4 or by picking Highlights and Notes from the View menu. Note that if you add arrows and shapes to a document, they're not included in this list.

Signing forms

A 'digital signature' can mean maths code used to verify files and transactions, but Preview takes care of a more basic need: to paste a copy of your handwritten signature into a PDF, such as a form that you need to sign.

Start by signing your name on a piece of white paper using a black pen. Make sure it's an accurate representation of your signature, has good contrast and isn't too fine to see clearly; once digitised, it can be used again and again.

In Preview, open Preferences by pressing Cmd-, (comma) and go to the Signatures tab. Click Create Signature and hold up the paper with your signature on it to your MacBook's iSight camera, aligning the bottom of the signature with the blue baseline shown. It'll be reversed in the camera view, so use the monochrome preview to the right to help you reposition it until it fits within the available area. When it does, click Accept.

Now close Preferences and open a document you want to sign. Scroll down to where you want your signature and click the Signature button on the Edit toolbar. The cursor will switch to a cross-hair. Use this to drag out the signature to size.

You can store multiple signatures in the same way, and pick the one you want each time.

Image editing

Preview also provides image editing tools. Because these are powered by features built into OS X's Core Image processing layer, they'll look familiar if you've used Apple's iPhoto or Aperture picture management apps.

At its simplest, Preview makes it easy to downsize an image, via Tools > Adjust size, or crop it, using the crop tool on the right of the Edit toolbar (again, reveal this using the Show Edit Toolbar button, with the pencil icon). The toolbar gains new options when you open an image.

The first four of these image tools handle selections: click and drag to marquee a rectangle, ellipse or freeform area, to which any adjustments will then apply. Smart Lasso selects contiguous matching colours as you drag across the image, a bit like Photoshop's Quick Selection tool, though

↑ **Preview's slider-operated image adjustment controls harness capabilities built into OS X.**

↑ TextEdit can be used in Plain Text mode for code editing or Rich Text for word processing tasks.

not as controllable. The next tool, Instant Alpha, works similarly to Smart Lasso but makes the area you drag over transparent; it's first highlighted in red, then removed with a tap of the Backspace key.

Click the Adjust Color button, second from the right, to pop up Preview's colour correction tools in a floating panel that Apple calls a heads-up display, or HUD. Its sliders are deceptively capable, with adjustments for exposure, sharpness and saturation, separate controls for shadows and highlights, and a smart Tint tool that removes false colour casts: click anywhere that ought to be neutral grey.

For a quick fix, skip all of these sliders and click Auto Levels at the top, immediately below the histogram display. This balances out the tones in the image so that the luminance is evenly spread between extreme shadow (black) and extreme highlight (white).

You can achieve a similar effect with more control by dragging the black and white handles below the histogram inwards to the points where the ends of the coloured area fall to the baseline. Drag the grey handle that sits between them to adjusts the overall bias or 'gamma' of the image, making midtones appear paler or deeper.

TextEdit is a very basic word processor that's provided with OS X. You'll probably want something more powerful for serious work, such as Apple's Pages (part of the iWork suite and available cheaply from the Mac App Store), Microsoft Word or one of the many third-party word processors on the market, but TextEdit has everything you need to get by.

Plain vs rich text

On the Format menu, you can choose whether to work with plain text, which is shown in a monospaced font, or 'rich text', where you can apply styles and formatting, set up the page size and margins, and change the typeface, size and colour. The Font palette, brought up by Cmd-T, also appears elsewhere in OS X.

TextEdit can open and edit common formats such as Microsoft Word's .doc and .docx files, although some advanced features may not appear. To open a file containing HTML/CSS code for editing, tick 'Ignore rich text commands' in the dialog box that appears when you press Cmd+O, so that TextEdit shows you the source code rather than displaying the content that it generates.

iMovie and GarageBand

Apple's creative apps are one of the reasons people choose Macs – video editing and music-making come as standard with every model.

Every Mac comes with a suite of simple, powerful creative apps known as iLife, comprising GarageBand, iMovie and iPhoto. We'll look at iPhoto on p86. At the time of writing, the current releases are still known as iMovie '11 and GarageBand '11, but in fact both have been substantially upgraded since that year, with plenty of clever new features and more integration with the companion apps on iOS, which work on iPad, iPhone and iPod touch.

↑ **The iLife apps are available for OS X and iOS.**

Easy editing

Movie editing can be a daunting task, so **iMovie** works hard to make it simpler without limiting your options. The first step is to grab some video footage, and iMovie supports a very wide range of formats, including tape-based MiniDV cameras (connected via FireWire, also known as i.Link, available on older MacBooks or with an adaptor from Apple for newer models),

modern AVCHD camcorders, MPEG-4 and H.264 video files from compact and DSLR cameras, action cameras such as the GoPro HERO3, and of course video from your iPhone or iPad. Or you can shoot straight into iMovie from the iSight camera on your MacBook or a connected webcam.

Having imported some clips, it's easy to drag them into iMovie's timeline and tweak their start and end points by clicking and dragging. Hundreds

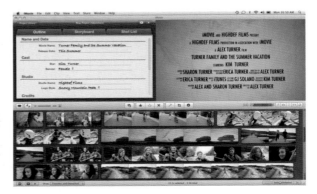

↑ **iMovie's timeline allows detailed, precise editing – or for some quick fun, build your own Trailer.**

↑ GarageBand lets you combine audio recordings with software instruments, loops and effects.

of special effects and transitions are on tap, and you also have full control over audio, including the audio channels on your clips and any external sound, voiceovers or music you want to add. The level of control is very detailed, yet it's also easy to figure out what to do, because most edits can be made by clicking on what you want to change. iMovie also helps organise your material, with tools including People Finder, which uses facial recognition to categorise clips by who's in them.

For a quick and impressive result from home movie footage, the recently introduced Trailers feature is perfect. Instead of editing from scratch, choose from more than a dozen templates to quickly build a short production in genres such as adventure, drama or romantic comedy, with clips, stylish titles and credits, and an epic soundtrack.

 **GarageBand** is a music production app that can be used to develop ideas or produce finished tracks. Hundreds of built-in software instruments can be played from a connected USB keyboard or other digital instrument, or you can record real instruments and vocals through your MacBook's built-in mic or external kit. There are virtual amps for electric guitarists and a vast range of effects. Apple Loops, ready-made clips of music, vocals and Foley, cover whatever you can't create from scratch, with thousands more available in the Audio Units format. Like iMovie, GarageBand makes it easy to get started but won't limit you too much as your ambitions grow, with as many tracks as you need and pro features like rhythm matching.

iPhoto

Everyone takes digital photos, so this comprehensive and attractive image management app could become one of your most-used tools.

These days even the casual snapper will build up an enormous collection of photos without even trying, and the best way to preserve and enjoy them all is to regularly transfer them to your Mac and keep them properly organised. With Time Machine active, you'll also know there's a backup of your memories – although it's wise to burn your favourites to DVD now and again, or upload them to a remote web server or an online service such as Flickr, in case physical disaster strikes your study.

Importing pictures

There are several ways to get new photos into iPhoto. You can make the app appear whenever you connect your camera or iPhone: to set this up, press Cmd-, (comma) or choose Preferences from the iPhoto menu while running iPhoto, click the General tab and use the drop-down menu labelled 'Connecting camera opens' to select iPhoto. Or launch iPhoto from the Dock and find your camera or phone under Devices in the left-hand column of its main window. You can also drag files or folders onto iPhoto's window, or use File > Import to Library (Cmd-Shift-I) to load

from any storage location. iPhoto supports most image file formats, and will manage, display and edit camera raw files, though it can't save edits back to raw, only to JPEG or TIF.

The best and most reliable way to use iPhoto is to allow it to make copies of all the images it manages and store them inside the iPhoto Library file. By default, this lives inside the Pictures folder in your home folder within Users on your Macintosh HD. It looks like a single file, and you can't open it like a folder by double-clicking – that just takes you into iPhoto. But if you want to see inside it, right-click it and choose Show Package Contents. Then it opens up just like a folder, with subfolders containing all your pictures organised in iPhoto's own way.

↓ You can choose how iPhoto handles image storage and editing.

↑ **Even without any effort on your part, iPhoto will organise pictures by time, place and people.**

Never rearrange these files or open them in another app for editing – you'll confuse iPhoto and could end up losing pictures. They are ordinary Mac files, though, so if anything does ever go horribly wrong with iPhoto itself, your images will still be there and can be imported into a new install of iPhoto or another app altogether.

If you prefer to keep your iPhoto Library somewhere else, perhaps to save space on your startup drive, you can: close iPhoto (by using File > Quit within the app or right-clicking its Dock icon and choosing Quit), then drag the iPhoto Library to another storage location, and finally double-click the iPhoto Library to let iPhoto know where it is; it should open normally.

Alternatively, if you go to the Advanced tab in iPhoto's Preferences and untick 'Copy items to the iPhoto Library', any image files you import will stay where they are, and iPhoto will just show you them and let you organise them within the app. This allows you to keep all your pictures in a folder structure of your choosing on an internal or external hard drive while managing them through

iPhoto. But take care to copy files into your folders before importing them: if you unthinkingly import straight from a camera memory card, then erase it, iPhoto won't have your pictures. That's why we recommend using the iPhoto Library.

A quick way to organise photos is to create an album, by pressing Cmd-N, and drag photos from the main window onto it in the sidebar.

 Another way to get images into iPhoto is via Photo Stream (see p110). This feature of iCloud stores the last 1,000 photos taken using any of the Macs and iOS devices on your iCloud account and displays them on all the others (subject to your settings). So once you enable it via iPhoto > Preferences > Photo Stream, you won't have to connect your iPhone to your Mac in future and import the pictures you've taken – they'll appear in iPhoto as soon as they're transferred over the internet from your iPhone.

Be aware, though, that when you see a picture in iPhoto's Photo Stream, that doesn't mean

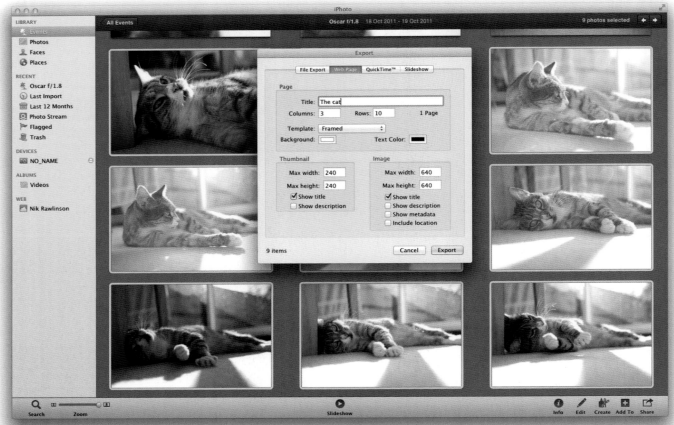

↑ **Although iPhoto lacks the web gallery features of MobileMe, iCloud's predecessor, you can export a set of photos as a simple web page, which you can then upload to your server if you wish.**

it's permanently stored on your Mac. You can tick Automatic Import (in Preferences) to make that happen, or leave it unticked and remember to manually select photos in Photo Stream that you want to keep, right-click and import them.

Faces   People are often the most important elements in everyday photos, and iPhoto uses facial recognition to spot who they are. It's pretty good at knowing when it sees the same person twice, but of course it won't know that person's name until you tell it.

Assuming you've imported some images by now, click the Faces item in iPhoto's left sidebar. Faces that iPhoto has detected are arranged as a series of Polaroids on a cork pinboard, with the name of each person written beneath the image. It looks a bit like a scene from a police procedural drama, but it's not that sinister. To get the benefit, every time you import a new set of photos that

includes shots of people (or periodically, if you're importing automatically via Photo Stream), you should add them to Faces. To do this, click the Find Faces graphic at the bottom of the Faces window. iPhoto will present some faces for you to name.

↑ **The Faces view presents everyone iPhoto has found in your photos so far, so you can quickly find all the pictures of someone.**

↑ Identify a face once; iPhoto will find it again.

The number of images displayed is determined by the size of the app window, so make it as big as you can. In the screenshot above, iPhoto has found a face but doesn't know who it is, so it's showing an 'unnamed' tag. We've started typing the correct name into this. iPhoto has access to any names we've previously entered, and to our OS X Contacts, so it's correctly guessed that the name we're typing is Richard Gooding. You can press Return to confirm the choice at this point, or Tab to confirm it and move to the next face in the list you're looking at, for speed.

Once you've identified a face or two, iPhoto will start making guesses of its own for the identities of people in new photos. Click the tick beside a suggestion to confirm its guess, or the cross to clear the tag and type a name in yourself. Having identified each of the faces in a batch of photos, clicking Show More Faces at the bottom will call up the next set, until you've finished identifying all the faces detected so far.

Of course, iPhoto may detect the faces of random people who you don't want want to identify or spot again. Hover over each face that iPhoto has outlined with a white bounding box, and click the cross that appears on it to remove that face from the catalogue of possible matches.

Places Now that we're no longer easily impressed by ever-higher megapixel resolutions, camera manufacturers have started to think about what other features might put their products ahead of the competition. One of the most useful innovations they've come up with – and it's getting more common in every season's new cameras – is built-in GPS. Like iPhones and satnavs, cameras with this feature capture data broadcast by global positioning satellites to work out the coordinates of their location. They then write these into the metadata of each image you shoot.

Apps including iPhoto, Apple's Aperture and Adobe Photoshop Lightroom, as well as photo sharing sites such as Flickr, can use this data to position your shots on a map, so you can see where you've been and browse pictures by location. All you have to do to use this feature in iPhoto is import pictures in the usual way; if they contain GPS data, it'll be used. Click Places in the sidebar to check that it's working, and you should see each picture you've taken with a GPS-enabled device represented on the map with a red pushpin.

↓ Quite naturally, iPhoto is liable to confuse parents with their children – but it can learn.

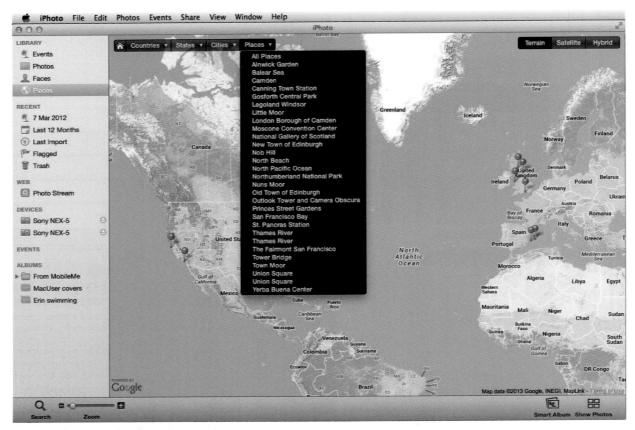

↑ **When you take pictures with GPS-enabled devices, iPhoto can automatically plot them on a map.**

If this isn't happening, go to the Advanced tab in iPhoto's Preferences, as on p86, and make sure 'Look up places' is set to 'Automatically' (rather than 'Never'). The option below, 'Include location information for published photos', refers to the data that's included when you make photos visible to others from iPhoto, in ways we'll see.

The Places feature depends on an active internet connection, since iPhoto downloads its map data from remote servers, enabling it to show the same kinds of plan, satellite and hybrid views that you'd expect from Apple Maps or Google Maps.

Your iPhone, along with most smartphones, is among the GPS-equipped devices you might be taking pictures with – but it'll only record location data if it's permitted to. In iOS, go to Settings > Privacy > Location Services and make sure both the slider at the top of the screen, beside Location Services, and the one beside Camera are set to On. If you have a 3G or Cellular iPad model, it's also GPS-equipped, and even Wi-Fi iPads and iPod

touch models, which don't have a GPS chip, will store your location via Location Services if you tell them to – they just may not be as accurate.

If your camera doesn't have GPS, or you have a lot of older photos from before such things were commonplace, you can still tag each picture with a location manually. The quickest way is by Event.

↑ **No GPS? Just tell iPhoto where you were.**

Events Events are simply sets of pictures that iPhoto lumps together because they were taken at about the same time. Click Events in the sidebar, highlight an Event stack and click the 'i' button on the bottom toolbar, or press Cmd-I. This calls up a metadata sidebar on the right in which you can add a short description and set the key photo that's used to depict the Event in the library: hover over the thumbnail at the top of the sidebar, move (don't drag) left and right, then click when you find the image you want to use.

With an Event – or, if you prefer, individual photos – selected, you can add these to the Places map using the Location panel, which sits at the bottom of the right-hand sidebar. Start typing the name of the place where you took the photo(s) where it says 'Assign a place', and iPhoto will search its database for matches. If it can't find any, it'll go to Apple's remote servers for a bigger list.

The more letters you type, the more refined the result will be. When you have the correct location, or the nearest place you can get iPhoto to recognise, it'll drop a pin at that spot. Clicking the pin on the map reveals the name of the place, with a shortcut chevron beside it that, when clicked, shows the associated photos in a thumbnail view.

Keywords Something else you can do in the Info sidebar, accessed by pressing Cmd-I, is add keywords to a selected photo. Just type words into

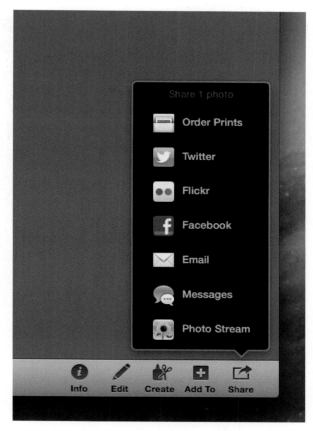

↑ **iPhoto offers lots of ways to share pictures.**

the box below 'Keywords'. To see all the keywords you've ever added, press Cmd-K. To search by keyword – or any other criteria – use the search box at the bottom left. The main window updates to display only photos matching what you enter.

Sharing At the bottom right of iPhoto's window is the Share icon, found across both OS X and iOS. Click this to open a Share Sheet listing all the currently available sharing options. Pick Order Prints and Apple will send you physical copies of the selected photos, at sizes of your choice, within about a week. (If you fancy something more ambitious, from the File menu you can create and order beautiful photo books, calendars and cards).

The options to send photos to Twitter (one at a time), Flickr, Facebook, email and Messages are self-explanatory. Pick Photo Stream to create a Shared Photo Stream, via iCloud, that you can then make public to anyone with a web browser.

APERTURE SCIENCE

If you need an app like iPhoto, but work with large volumes of pictures and need to manage and tweak raw images from pro cameras, you'll be better off with a more advanced app such as Apple's Aperture, available from the App Store, or Adobe's Photoshop Lightroom, which you can buy alone or as part of a Creative Cloud subscription. Which you prefer is really a matter of personal taste.

iWork

Pages, Numbers and Keynote are Apple's equivalents of Microsoft Word, Excel and PowerPoint – except that they're much slicker.

The three iWork apps aren't included with your Mac, but they're quick and cheap to buy from the Mac App Store. There are also iOS editions and – just announced at the time of writing – a web version, iWork for iCloud, accessible from PCs.

 Pages, Apple's word processor, is deliberately not as heavy with features as Word, but it covers the main functions most of us use, including track changes, table of contents and footnotes as well as all the obvious formatting features. Its Page Layout mode, comparable to Word's Publishing Layout View but less clunky, handles desktop publishing tasks too. Pages uses its own .pages file format, but can import Word files with reasonable success and can export to Word, .RTF and PDF. It's also a good tool for creating ebooks in the standard ePub format.

Pages looks and works similarly to the iLife apps. A large, simple toolbar at the top gives you access to its most common features, and an

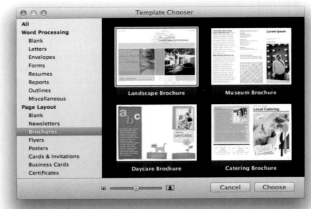

↑ **Page Layout documents work more like DTP.**

Inspector palette (accessed by clicking the blue 'i' towards the right) lets you make changes to your document and pull in resources from iPhoto and iTunes. Notice how all iPhoto's organisational aids, such as Events and Places, are accessible here, as are the Faces you've identified and your albums.

Like other good word processors, Pages encourages you to set up styles – collections of attributes, such as font, size and spacing – which

Add sheets and tables   **Data management**   **Add document elements**   **Open control palettes**

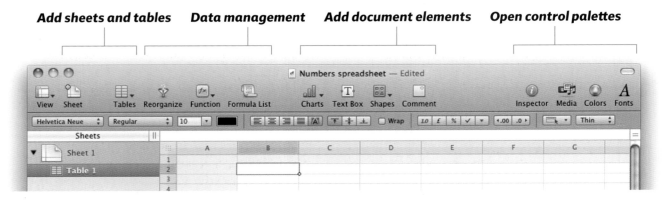

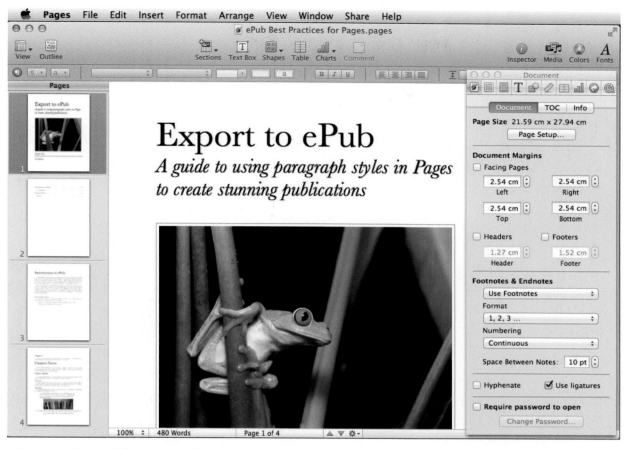

↑ Pages suits a wide variety of document preparation tasks, with plenty of advanced features.

you can then apply to sections of text to achieve consistent styling, especially in long documents.In Pages, make a new document by clicking Cmd-N, press Return to choose the default Blank template, and click the small, round blue icon at the far left of the toolbar, marked with a paragraph sign (¶). This opens the Styles drawer. Type a few words onto your blank page, and they'll appear by default in the Normal style.

Select some of your text and choose a new font from the toolbar. Now the downward-pointing triangle beside Normal in the drawer turns red, indicating that the selected text no longer matches the style applied. Click the triangle and you can choose Revert to Defined Style to return the selected paragraph to Normal style, or Redefine Style from Selection to change the Normal style – and any other Normal paragraphs in this document – to the same specification as your selected text.

Get into the habit of applying styles to text – best of all, styles with meaningful names, such as Body (for the main text or story of a document), Heading and Subheading – and you'll be able to tweak the look of your document very quickly at any time, altering every subheading, for example, just by updating the style applied to all of them.

When you make a new document, notice that the templates are divided between Word Processing and Page Layout types; these aren't interchangeable, so decide if you want continuous text with pictures appearing where they fall, as in a report or ebook, or fixed pages or spreads with everything placed in position, like a magazine.

When you press Cmd-S or go to File > Save, Pages will save your document in its own format. To pass it on to others who don't use Pages, use Share > Export to save in Word or RTF format. To preserve the exact appearance, choose PDF, but you'll only be able to view this version, not edit it.

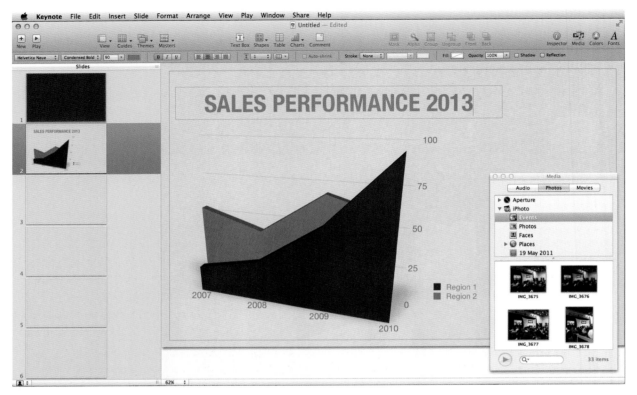

↑ **Keynote is the software Apple created for Steve Jobs' presentations, so you know it'll be neat.**

Numbers, Apple's spreadsheet, takes a notably different approach from Excel, although if you've used one it's not hard to get to grips with the other. It's more flexible and more attractive, not least thanks to its charts, which are far smoother than Microsoft's.

One of Numbers' biggest innovations is that you can have more than one table on any sheet. Open Numbers (see p92), press Cmd-N and pick Blank to make an empty document. At the left is a column showing the sheets in the document and tables on each sheet. At the right, you'll see grey cells across the top and down the left of the active table. Now right-click on Table 1 in the sidebar and select Delete. The cells disappear, but Sheet 1 remains. Click the Tables button and select Sums Checklist. A new table appears in Sheet 1, with tick boxes that let you mark off items. Enter some details in columns B and C, then tick a few boxes to the left. Notice how the total at the foot of column C doesn't start to rack up until you tick the boxes in column A – just one of Numbers' handy

predefined functions. Now add another table… and another. Move and resize them (drag the bottom right corner). You can't do this in Excel!

Keynote, Apple's legendary presentation app, serves the same purpose as PowerPoint without the clutter and hideous presets. It's brilliant if you don't have a lot of design experience – and even better if you do. The 36 predesigned themes each come in five screen sizes and provide a wide variety of slide templates, accessed from the Masters button in the toolbar. If you change your mind about the look, you can swap themes and all your slides will update.

The gorgeous ready-made elements are complemented by superb layout tools and powerful graphing. The View menu at the left of the toolbar flips you between slide creation and navigation modes, a light table to organise your slides, and the Presenter Notes view, which will help you through your talk on your MacBook while the audience sees only your slides on a second screen.

Microsoft Office

It's one of the reasons people want to escape the PC world… but if you do need Office, there's a 'different yet equal' version for OS X.

Although it's now firmly associated with Windows, Microsoft Office first appeared way back in 1985 on the Mac. The Mac version remains a distinct but similarly capable product, with each offering a few features that the other lacks and vice versa. The biggest difference is that Microsoft's **Access** database doesn't exist on the Mac (the equivalent being FileMaker, made by a subsidiary of Apple). But perhaps the most important point is that file compatibility is excellent, with very little chance of anything coming adrift when exchanging files between PC and Mac – especially now Microsoft's large set of Office fonts is common to both platforms.

Word and **Excel** remain the world's most popular word processor and spreadsheet, and their native file formats are used by many other apps. This was complicated when Microsoft switched to XML-based formats (.docx and so on), but those too are now supported by many other apps – which means it's by no means essential to use Office itself. But Word's notebook view and excellent outlining are unique selling points.

Excel rules the corporate world, and the hassle of converting reams of complex existing spreadsheets to another app may not be justifiable, so this is a common reason to go with Office. And **PowerPoint** – well, everyone knows PowerPoint, but Keynote is increasingly seen as the pro presenter's weapon of choice.

Outlook, the email app, is included only with the more expensive Home and Business version of Office. There's no reason to choose it over Mail except compatibility with enterprise systems.

Office is also available as Office 365 Home Premium, 'software in the cloud' for a monthly fee.

↑ Outlook is among the familiar apps available in Office for Mac 2011.

Apple's Pro apps

Macs have long been the favourite of creative professionals, and Apple woos them with high-end apps at affordable prices.

 While Apple's operating systems and consumer apps are second to none, it's not traditionally a major player in pro software, leaving specialist tools to the likes of Adobe and upmarket niche players. But with the launch of Final Cut Pro in 1999, exclusively for the Mac, it demonstrated how groundbreaking software could help to sell its hardware, cutting the cost of a serioius non-linear editing suite overnight by as much as 90%.

Final Cut continued to build a solid user base among broadcast and film editors until 2011, when Apple made an equally dramatic move by completely redesigning the software in the form of **Final Cut Pro X** and moving it into the Mac App

↑ **Motion complements FCP X with animation.**

Store, with another huge price cut. This made it cheaper than far less capable rivals, and Apple discontinued its own Final Cut Express to make room. But the pros weren't looking for price cuts, and some of the changes, in particular the omissions of key requirements for industry workflows, were too much for high-end users to stomach. A migration began to alternatives such as Adobe Premiere and Avid Media Composer, despite their higher prices.

This tide seems to be turning back as FCP regains features, and for anyone setting up a video studio on a budget, an iMac or Retina MacBook Pro with FCP X remains an exceptionally affordable and credible combination.

↑ **Apple's Logic Pro 9 is as good a music production app as you can get.**

↑ The powerful 15in MacBook Pro with Retina display is a perfect platform for Final Cut Pro X.

The arrival of the new Mac Pro should throw a different light again on FCP X as a feature film editing option.

Many of the features typically provided by external apps are built into FCP X, including effects, titles, keyframing, chroma keying, audio editing and colour grading. Motion graphics, including advanced titling, transitions and effects, are handled by a separate but even cheaper app, Motion, while high-end video encoding is provided by the similarly priced Compressor.

The other Apple app that carries a 'Pro' designation is **Logic Pro**, the DAW (digital audio work-station) package. Learning from the success of Final Cut, Apple bought Logic from its maker, Emagic, in 2002, and immediately discontinued the Windows version, substantially enhancing the Mac version to attract creative users to its platform. By 2004 it looked and felt like a native OS X app. In 2011, Logic Pro

9 followed Final Cut Pro into the Mac App Store, with MainStage, a companion app for live audio performance that can also be used by itself, becoming available as a separate low-cost product.

Logic is a comprehensive and notably attrac-tive app, having gained some of the 'gingerbread' from GarageBand, including a glossy interactive timeline and finely crafted visual representations of virtual instruments and equipment. It remains a solid rival to other DAWs such as Avid Pro Tools, Propellerhead Reason and Steinberg Cubase. At the time of writing, though, it was feeling a little unloved by Apple; it remains to be seen whether and when the next upgrade is forthcoming.

Finally, although not labelled 'Pro', **Aperture** is very much aimed at professionals. Many photogra-phers swear by its high-volume workflow and management features and raw editing facilities, but Adobe's Lightroom provides stiff competition.

Adobe Creative Cloud

Adobe's Creative Suite has dominated the graphics and interactive industries for years. Now, controversially, it's subscription-only.

If there's one app that you can rely on almost every creative professional having on their hard disk, it's Photoshop. For some time, Adobe has built on its popularity by offering it in bundles with well regarded but less ubiquitous graphics, web design, animation and video editing apps, giving better value for money, though still adding up to an investment straying up into four figures.

In 2012, however, Adobe put a twist on Creative Suite by introducing Creative Cloud. The software itself didn't move to the cloud, except in the sense that you could download it; the apps were still installed on your Mac's hard disk. The difference was that instead of buying a set of apps, then choosing whether to pay for upgrades or stick with what you had, you could opt to pay a monthly fee, with no big up-front cost, and get any future upgrades included.

Around half a million users took up the offer, but it still came as a shock when, in 2013, Adobe announced that the upcoming new versions of its apps (with a few exceptions, including Lightroom) would *only* be available on subscription. And while the pricing looks fair compared to the previous one-off cost, it's disconcerting that if you ever stop paying for your apps, they'll stop working. You can subscribe to just one app if that's all you need, although the Complete deal is better value; and there are discounts for students, but not as generous as those for the earlier boxed versions, especially considering you have to find the money for a full-price subscription when you leave college or lose your apps.

Adobe says it'll keep all of this under review, but won't be reversing the move to subscription. Whether or not it sounds like a good thing to you, the apps still lead the creative market, so chances are you'll be at least considering investing in them.

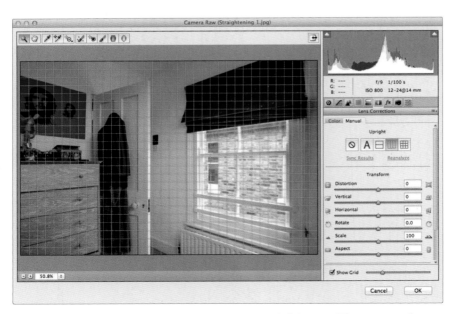

↑ **Photoshop now makes Camera Raw available as a filter to apply.**

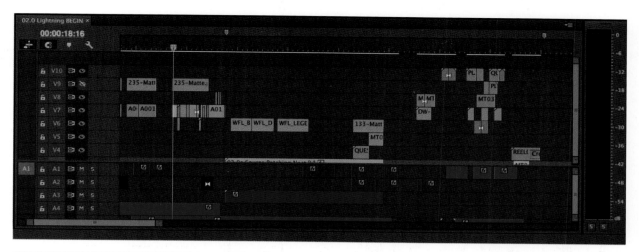

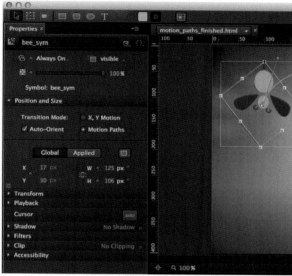

↑ **Premiere Pro gets a redesigned timeline.**

← **Could Edge Animate be Flash for a new era?**

Muse CC makes this recently introduced visual website creation app more flexible, and adds features like layers and parallax scrolling, but it still feels glitchy and unfinished.

Illustrator CC doesn't get the updates to graphing and 3D that users have waited more than a decade for, but gains a type smooshing tool and the ability to export graphics to CSS, which is certainly an attempt to move with the times.

Premiere Pro and **After Effects CC**, which compete with Apple's Final Cut Pro X and the likes of Avid, get some quite significant feature, performance and workflow improvements; Premiere has a revamped timeline and Retina support.

Flash Professional CC gets a new code editor and the ability to export Full HD video. The **Edge CC** web design tools, including Edge Animate, potentially a standards-based successor to Flash, continue to look interesting but deliver a limited amount. **Dreamweaver CC** spruces up the web design warhorse, but without finding a new direction that gives it a convincing future outside the more stolid enterprise environments.

Lightroom 5 – included if you take out a full CC subscription, but also available to buy alone – gains features including Smart Previews, so you can keep your full high-res images on an external drive at home and still view and edit the pics on your MacBook without the space overhead.

Photoshop CC remains unrivalled as an all-round image editor, although many users in web design and user interface work favour leaner apps such as Pixelmator and Acorn. This version gains Conditional Actions, which automate more complex operations; smarter image resizing and sharpening; Shake Reduction to correct camera movement; editable round-cornered rectangles; and the ability to apply Camera Raw tweaks while editing, rather than only in a separate module

InDesign CC gets what every publication designer has been waiting for: Retina support. A 15in MacBook Pro (with Retina display) becomes an effective machine for page layout at last. Not much else is new in this version, though, except for a revamped Font menu and a move to the dark grey user interface seen in other Adobe apps.

Games on the Mac

Macs are capable of running games just as well as PCs, and Apple's popularity is contributing to a steady rise in the number available.

Not many people would buy a Mac specifically to run games, largely because there've always been fewer titles available for OS X than for Windows. In turn, Apple, catering for the buyers it had rather than those who weren't interested anyway, has tended not to favour the kind of configuration gamers are often looking for – big boxes with modest core specs and dubious aesthetics but room for huge graphics cards. Many of today's Macs, though, are actually great for gaming, and while there's always the option of installing Windows (see p66) and running PC games, there's also a growing number of Mac titles available.

One reason for this is the Mac App Store, which has brought the iOS ethos to OS X: relatively small but high-quality entertainment products at low prices for the casual gamer. Another is Steam: Valve's gaming platform, accessed through its own storefront and code management app that verifies your installed games online to reduce software piracy, has brought dozens of major titles to the Mac, including classics such as the Half-Life and Portal series as well as newer releases.

When it comes to current games, companies like Feral Interactive have seen an opportunity in the resurgence of the Mac and are doing sterling work in bringing more PC titles across, from Sega Superstars Tennis to XCOM: Enemy Unknown. The Total War series combines turn-based strategy with real-time tactics for the kind of high-investment experience PC gamers traditionally love, while Lego The Lord of the Rings is irresistible in taking an utterly silly concept seriously enough to create a gorgeous and engaging game. And then there's the uniquely chilling BioShock series.

Game Center, first launched on iOS, has

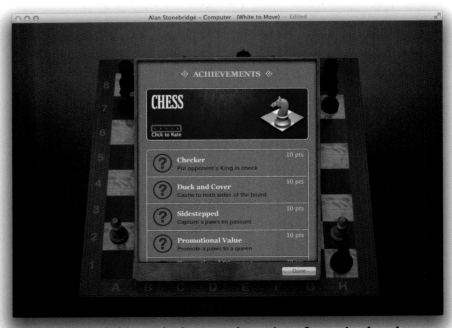

↑ Game Center's bizarrely decorated user interface raised eyebrows; OS X 10.9 slims it down, but will more games use it on the Mac?

↑ **Lego The Lord of the Rings features puzzle-solving, slapstick, dwarf-throwing, music and fun.**

also come to the Mac, giving game developers a standard means of storing and retrieving a user's progress and high scores. It's useful that Notification Center can displays an alert when it's your move in a turn-based game, and more excitingly, Game Center also enables multiplayer

gaming between OS X and iOS versions of a title. In practice, though, the uptake of Game Center has been far from universal as yet, and not many developers are taking advantage of its most advanced features. Notifications, meanwhile, are sometimes used by games merely to nag for attention, although they can be turned off.

↑ **Sonic and SEGA All-Stars Racing is a treat, with clever moves and a real sense of speed.**

Performance

If you're planning to buy a MacBook and have gaming in mind, a top-end MacBook Pro with a dedicated graphics card will obviously be the best choice. But even entry-level models such as the 11in MacBook Air, with its new Intel HD 5000 GPU and Haswell Core i5 CPU, shouldn't struggle except with the most demanding titles, as long as you don't mind turning advanced options down in 3D games to trade frame rate for quality.

With iMacs lacking user-upgradable graphics cards and the Mac Pro looking too expensive as a leisure machine except for the inordinately affluent gamer, it seems unlikely the Mac will become the dominant gaming format in the near future – but that doesn't mean you shouldn't enjoy many hours of rewarding play.

Chapter 4
iCloud

iCloud and iOS devices

Apple's online service mostly works out of sight, keeping everything synced between your Mac, iPhone and other Apple equipment.

iCloud is many things. It's the brains behind Siri on the iPhone and Dictation on the Mac, sending your speech to Apple's servers and getting a response in a split second. It's the tool that underpins your Apple ID, remembering every app and piece of content you've bought from Apple and syncing them between your Macs, iOS devices and Apple TV. It's an email service with an attractive webmail interface. It's your online address book, synced calendar and Photo Stream. It's how games remember your high scores. It's an automatic backup service for iOS and a central document repository for OS X.

So, quite useful, then. iCloud is truly indispensable if you have a Mac and another Apple device, or several of both; but even if you only have a Mac, it enables many of the convenience features that enhance OS X.

You don't need to create an iCloud account: it happens automatically when you activate iCloud on any device with your Apple ID. If you've ever bought anything from iTunes, the email and password you used to log in is your Apple ID. If you don't have an Apple ID, set one up at appleid.apple.com. Then open System Preferences on your Mac, from the Dock or the Apple menu. Click iCloud, turn iCloud on and log in with

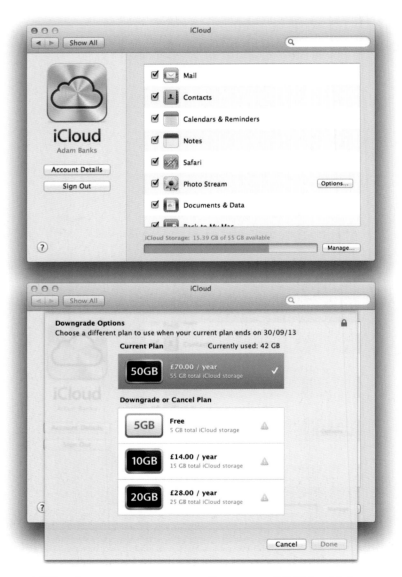

↑ **iCloud supports numerous features of OS X, which you can activate in System Preferences. But if you run out of room, extra server space can get quite expensive.**

your Apple ID. Then you can tick whichever iCloud services you want to use on this machine. There's usually no reason not to tick all of them, unless you're having a problem with something and need to try turning it off.

Storage space

Your free iCloud account comes with 5GB of free storage on Apple's servers. 5GB isn't nothing, but considering Flickr offers every user 1,000GB, Apple's offer doesn't sound very generous. Keep in mind, though, that

↑ **Your iTunes purchases, iTunes Match collection, apps and Photo Stream don't count against your storage allocation. But your Camera Roll does, and backing up iOS devices is likely to take up the most space. OS X apps can also save more documents than you expected.**

your 5GB will be eaten into only by documents and backups you choose to store 'in the cloud'. Although iCloud keeps track of all your apps and iTunes music and movie purchases, and passes up to 1,000 pictures around between your Macs and devices in your Photo Stream, none of that counts towards your data allowance. The apps and iTunes purchases are already stored on Apple's servers, so you're not taking up any extra space by having purchased them. Your Photo Stream will use server space, but Apple made the decision when it launched the feature that it would absorb the storage and bandwidth requirements.

So you probably won't fill up that 5GB as quickly as you think. Then again, if you have several iOS devices and they're all set to back up to iCloud – which is a sensible choice, because it makes it very easy to recover all your data if anything happens to your device – or if you do make heavy use of iCloud for document storage and transfer, you might find you need more room. Apple has a variety of paid upgrade levels; to see what's available to you, click iCloud in System Preferences, click the Manage button at the bottom right, then click Change Storage Plan.

Unfortunately, the upgrades, to a maximum of 50GB, come at quite expensive annual fees. In the same place in iCloud System Preferences, you can try to avoid the need for more storage by spotting what's using up a lot of space. iOS device backups are often the main culprit, but from iCloud System Preferences on your Mac you can't see exactly what elements within an iOS backup are taking up so much space. To do that, tap Settings on that device's home screen, then go to General > Usage and under iCloud tap Manage Storage. Tap the relevant backup to see a list of items and their size.

Note that where apps are listed here, it's not the apps themselves that

↑ Check the contents of your iOS device back-ups and you'll find what's eating your iCloud.

are being backed up – that would be pointless, since Apple already has a copy of every iOS app, which it can give you back if you have to restore your device. Rather, iCloud is backing up the unique data – files, settings and so on – that the app has generated on your device.

The largest item here is quite likely to be the Camera Roll, because we all take pictures all the time and there's no incentive to delete them. Well, if you've just looked up the prices of iCloud

storage, you have an incentive. The way to do it is to carefully import all the photos from the device into your iPhoto Library (see p86) or to a folder on your Mac via Image Capture (see p62). Then, once they're safe, delete them from the device. Tap photos, then Camera Roll, then Edit; tick images until your finger gets tired, tap Delete, and repeat in batches until finished. (Alternatively, use the option in iPhoto or Image Capture to delete images after importing, if you're sure.)

Then, on the device, go to Settings > iCloud > Storage & Backup and tap Back Up Now. Your backup will be overwritten with a new one that doesn't contain those gigabytes of photos, and you may not need to upgrade your iCloud storage after all – for now.

Contacts, Calendars and Notes

If you have a MacBook and an iPhone – or any other combination of Apple kit, really – it's very handy to have appointments that you set up, contacts that you add and virtual sticky notes that you write all synced automatically betwen them. iCloud can handle that without any fuss at all – just switch on the relevant options in your iCloud settings on all your machines, making sure to set them all up using the same Apple ID.

After a bit of tweaking by Apple to convert OS X to the iOS way of doing things, Macs, iPhones and iPads now all have apps called Calendar, Contacts, Notes and Reminders. The apps even look fairly similar, but you do get some extra features on the Mac compared to iOS. For example, double-click a note in the Notes app and it'll open in a separate window, which you can keep pinned to the Desktop if you like as a physical reminder, just like on your real desk. Notes can't be made to stay in front of other windows, though (the Stickies app does that, but annoyingly it won't sync over iCloud). Notes can be grouped into folders to make a long list manageable.

The Reminders app in OS X makes it easy to manage to-do lists. To save space, its sidebar can be hidden and you can swipe between lists. As in iOS, reminders can be set to appear when you

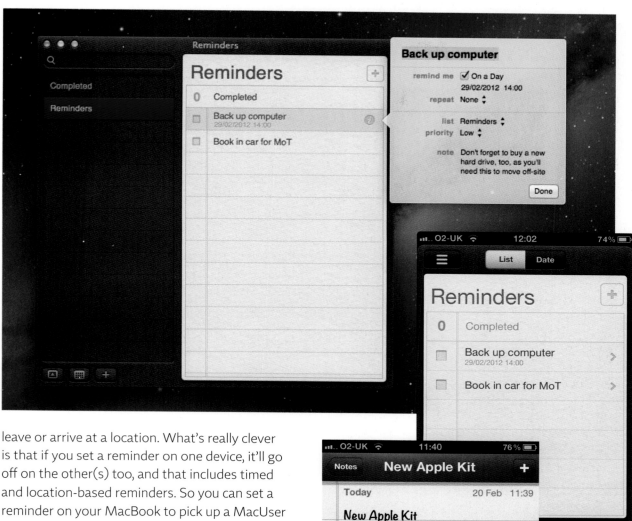

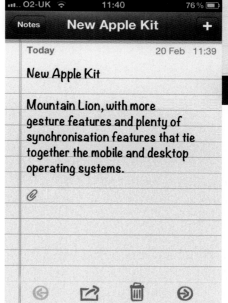

leave or arrive at a location. What's really clever is that if you set a reminder on one device, it'll go off on the other(s) too, and that includes timed and location-based reminders. So you can set a reminder on your MacBook to pick up a MacUser when you're at the station, then leave your Mac at home and arrive at the station with your iPhone, and your iPhone will give you the reminder. It should work the other way around, too, but the iPhone will be better at detecting its location.

As you'd expect, the same kind of seamless syncing applies to Calendar appointments.

iCloud Tabs When you're looking for something on the internet, you're likely to end up with a lot of Safari tabs open as you track it down, perhaps with useful information available in several of them. But the next time you have a few minutes to get on with your research, you may be on a different device – say, your iPad rather than your MacBook – so you'll have to go and find all of those URLs again. To avoid this frustration,

↑ As you fill in a Reminder on your Mac, it's already appearing on your iPhone. The same goes for Calendar entries and Notes – all thanks to iCloud.

↑ iCloud Tabs are now a feature of Safari on both OS X and iOS. Click the button to see what tabs are open on your other Macs and devices, so you needn't lose track.

both the OS X and iOS versions of Safari now tell iCloud what tabs are currently open (they can be in tabs or in separate windows, it doesn't matter), and iCloud in turn relays this info to Safari on other Macs and devices on your account. So when you click or tap the iCloud icon in Safari on any Mac or device, it'll list the URLs being viewed in the others; tap one to go there. If you set Safari on your Mac to Private Browsing (from the Safari menu), however, none of its tabs will be reported via iCloud, even those that are already open.

Documents in the Cloud

iCloud's seamless syncing activities are welcome, but a whole different use of cloud storage is to keep documents remotely, accessible at all times to all apps on all devices. Apple calls this 'Documents in the Cloud', and it's being introduced gradually, but several of OS X's default apps, including TextEdit and Preview, support it. In fact, when you press Cmd-S to save a document, they'll assume you want to save it iCloud, and you'll need to switch to your Mac's hard drive if that was where you intended. If you leave an app without saving and closing your work, it'll automatically go to iCloud too, so you can resume work on it later.

When you press Cmd-O to open a document in one of these apps, you'll see the iCloud Document Library, as in the picture opposite. At the top left is a switch to go back to your Mac's local storage. The Document Library window is more responsive than a typical Mac Open dialog. You can group files into folders here by dragging one icon onto another, just like organising apps in Launchpad or on the iOS home screen. What won't help get you organised is that typing in the search bar here ignores the names of your folders and only looks for matching *documents*.

It's also awkward that the Document Library only shows files that belong to the app you're using. There's no global view to see everything you have in iCloud, or to bind related files from different apps. It all works fine if you have relatively few documents to deal with, but scales up poorly.

Documents on your local disks can be moved into the cloud by dragging them from the Finder and dropping them into an iCloud Document Library. For documents that you already have open in an iCloud-savvy app, choose Move To from the File menu or click the document's name in its title bar and choose Move to iCloud.

Adjuncts to iCloud

Adjuncts rather than alternatives, because iCloud is free and essential to various Apple features, so you'll be using it one way or another. But for online document storage and syncing, a more flexible option at the moment is Dropbox, used by more than 50 million people. It was conceived by MIT graduate Drew Houston as a solution to his habit of frequently forgetting to carry his USB drive. It didn't take him long to realise this was a service that third parties would pay to use too.

Install Dropbox on your Mac – or PC – as explained at dropbox.com, and it sets up a folder called Dropbox wherever you choose – by default, inside your home folder – which will hold your synchronised files. Dragging any file into this folder will upload it to the Dropbox server. A client app, which sits in the OS X menu bar, monitors changes instigated by other machines logged in to the same account and pulls them down to the same local folder.

To share a Dropboxed file with someone else, you can just right-click it and pick Share Dropbox Link to get a URL to pass on.

On the iPad and iPhone, a dedicated Dropbox app lets you view a wide range of file types straight from your Dropbox folders in the cloud, and open others in third-party apps.

You could even access your iPhoto library from another Mac by saving it in the synchronised Dropbox folder. Bear in mind, though, that if you frequently import a lot of images or edit those already in your Library, you'll pass a lot of data over your broadband connection doing this.

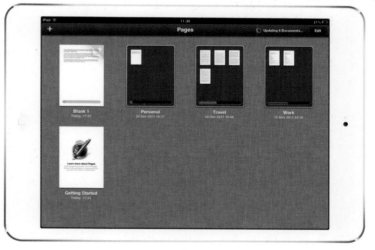

↑ **The iCloud Document Library appears in any compatible app in OS X or iOS, such as Pages. You'll only see files relevant to this app, not any others you may have put in the cloud. The blue progress bars on the thumbnails represent files that are still being uploaded. The turned corner with a white arrow on the document at the iPad's top left indicates that this file is waiting to sync to the cloud when you have a working internet connection.**

Photo Stream

Your latest 1,000 pictures, instantly available on all your Macs and iOS devices. It's a great idea, so make sure you get the most from it.

The first thing to note about Photo Stream is that it doesn't copy photos between your devices. What it does is see when you take a photo using any of your devices and then add it to a set of up to 1,000 images stored in the cloud. That set is then made visible on each of your devices over the internet – but the image file is still only stored on the device that originated the picture, and at some point you'll need to transfer it to a safer place. Once more than 1,000 images have been automatically added to Photo Stream, it'll keep ditching the oldest on a rolling basis, so they won't be displayed across your devices any more. It neither removes images from the device that originally took them, nor does it act as a backup of them.

Still, Photo Stream is very handy, especially if you have a small group of people all using the same devices on the same Apple ID regularly, whether in a family or a workgroup. A more recent addition, Shared Photo Streams, takes it a step further by allowing you to create your own mini Photo Streams of selected pictures. These don't expire in the same way, and you can share them with anyone you like, either privately or publicly.

Shared Photo Streams

To create a Shared Photo Stream, select some photos, click the Share button at the bottom right of iPhoto's window and choose Photo Stream. The Share Sheet changes to show any existing Shared Photo Streams; you can add the selected pics to one of these, making them available to the same audience, or click New to create another.

When making a new Shared Photo Stream, you're invited to enter the email addresses of people you want to share it with. These should be the email addresses associated with Apple users' iCloud accounts; your invitation will enable them to access your photo set from an OS X or iOS device associated with that same iCloud account.

→ **Creating a Shared Photo Stream works the same way from iPhoto in OS X as it does from Photos in iOS, although the apps are quite different**

↑ **Turn Photo Stream on to see it in iPhoto. You can receive the stream without adding pics to it.**

If you want people who don't necessarily use Apple products to see your photos, or to be able to post a URL for anyone to find, you need to tick the Public Website box. (It's then up to you whether you enter people's email addresses here so that they receive a link, or notify them another way.) This means the gallery will be created as a normal web page, omitting the ability for users to comment on the pictures or see others' comments. Using Apple IDs means users are identified, which Apple seems to think means they won't post irrelevant or offensive comments.

When you click Share, you'll be given a URL for the public website that's being created, which you can pass on to others. As the description suggests, your pictures will be openly available without any security, but as long as they're not of a particularly private nature that shouldn't really be an issue – it's unlikely anyone without the URL is going to stumble on them.

Your Photo Stream can also be viewed on a Windows PC with iCloud Control Panel installed. It's free to download from support.apple.com/kb/DL1455 and enables other sync features too.

↓ **Your Photo Stream is accessible on all your devices via iCloud, and any of them can initiate a Shared Photo Stream.**

Chapter 5
Accessories

AViiQ
Portable Laptop Stand

This ultra-slim, ultra-light aluminium MacBook stand looks like a simple piece of origami. It's a single flat sheet that folds into a prism at one end. Stand your Mac on it and you've got a more ergonomic typing angle, better airflow to cool the processors, and nothing to pack up and carry around except a 3mm thick sheet weighing just 350g. Minimalism at its best.

£34.95 from store.apple.com/uk
See aviiq.com for details

Cooler Master
JAS PRO

Here's some more smart thinking. The JAS PRO combines aluminium and rubber with positionable hinges to let you choose the angle at which to prop your MacBook, up to a steep rake to bring the screen nearer eye level. Its open design promotes cooling, and when not in use it folds flat – or you can fold your MacBook flat and prop it up to admire the Apple logo.

£47 from cmstore.eu (sold in Euros at €54.99)
See coolermaster-mobile.com for details

Twelve South
BookArc

Using your MacBook doesn't always mean using its screen and keyboard. Plugging in an external monitor and peripherals is a great way to harness its power while at your desk – but what do you do with the gently humming machine itself? Stand it up proudly in this mini Millennium Bridge of silicone-cushioned aluminium, that's what. It even tidies your cables.

£39.99 from amazon.co.uk
See twelvesouth.com for details

Moshi
ClearGuard and PalmGuard

Apple builds its notebook computers tougher than most, with their all but indestructible aluminium unibody and over-engineered hinges. But even if you're unlikely to make one fall apart, it still only takes a *grande latte* in the wrong place to zap its innards. Depending on your working environment, level of clumsiness and insurance excess, it might be very well worth your while to invest in some protection. Hiding those beautiful Apple finishes goes against the grain, but Moshi specialise in high-fashion accessories, so they're hardly going to overlook the aesthetics. In fact, their unobtrusive cling-on covers are so respectful of the hardware that they're stocked in the Apple Store. The ClearGuard keyboard cover fits the MacBook's tile-style keys so snugly you can forget it's there. The PalmGuard shields the whole grime-prone front section, with a separate, optional TrackGuard for the Multi-Touch trackpad. And the iVisor range of washable screen protectors promise bubble-free fitting, glare reduction and a clear, sharp image.

£17.95 to £39.95 from store.apple.com/uk
See moshimonde.com for details

Sanho
HyperJuice 2

There are lots of cute battery cases around, but this is something else. The HyperJuice 2 holds a huge 100Wh of power when charged, enough to keep a MacBook going more than 24 hours; or, with two 12W USB ports free, share the juice with your iPad and iPhone. The aluminium casing allows repair and replacement of parts. Note that an extra cable or adaptor is required.

£234.95 from protronica.co.uk
See hypershop.com for details

Crumpler
Muli Backpack - M

Suitable for MacBooks up to 13in, this compact rucksack is made of, it says here, 1000D Chicken Tex Supreme nylon, with a Ripstop lining: look closely and you can see the gridlines of thicker thread that mean even if a tear starts, it won't get far. Air mesh padding on the back and slim bumpers on the straps ensure your comfort, and the dedicated laptop compartment closes with Velcro to avoid spills. It's urban and it's chic.

£99 from new.crumpler.eu/uk

be.ez
LE Reporter Air 13

There's not much point in getting a pencil-thin MacBook Air and stuffing it in a courier bag the size of a duvet. So the fashionistas at be.ez (they pronounce it 'be easy') have come up with the Reporter, an 'envelope-style' bag that mimics the slim form of the Air yet has room for other stuff too. This particular colour combination is Kingfisher; there are three more.

£47 from amazon.co.uk
See be-ez.com/le-reporter-air-13 for details

Speck
SeeThru for MacBook Pro

Polycarbonate was Apple's favourite material before aluminium, and here's a chance to wrap one around the other. Speck sells Mac shell cases (try saying that fast) in a wide range of finishes, but our favourite is this purely transparent one, letting the beauty shine through. The whole exterior of the clamshell is covered, except for a neat grille to let the heat out.

£25 and up from amazon.co.uk
See speckproducts.com for details

Booq
Mamba Courier 15

Finished in a waterproof fabric made from jute, this satchel is fully padded, with a comfortable strap and handle and a semi-structured feel. The strap hooks are a bit fiddly – no doubt pickpockets will agree – but once inside you'll love the luxurious deep red lining, which forms a safe zone for your 15in MacBook. There's also a full-size iPad compartment, room for papers and cables, and a pocket at the back. Nice.

£106 from booqbags.co.uk

Knomo
Kobe 15

The soft tan leather gives this classic bag the slouchy opulence of a member's club sofa. Magnets hold the flap without fuss, and beneath are two generous accessory pockets. There's a big compartment for work and sundries, then the MacBook section, protected by Knomo's unique high-density foam quilting. The back isn't leather, but it's neat and tough, with an extra pocket. We want one.

£215 from knomobags.com/uk

MacAlly
AirFolio

It seems obvious once you've seen it, but this is such a clever case format. Grippy plastic inserts lock your MacBook Air in place within the tough, metallic outer casing, which wraps around whatever angle your screen is tilted (including shut, of course) and protrudes just enough at each side to absorb knocks before they reach the unibody. Simple and smart.

£35.99 from amazon.co.uk
See macally-europe.com for details

WD My Book
Thunderbolt Duo 4TB

With Thunderbolt 2 arriving, Thunderbolt 1 must finally be mainstream. Twin hard disks like this, set up as a striped RAID array, can reach high speeds with the original interface, as found in current MacBooks, and WD has included a second port for daisychaining. Although its sustained transfer rates aren't the steadiest, this is a good drive for your desk.

£429.95 from store.apple.com/uk
See wdc.com for details

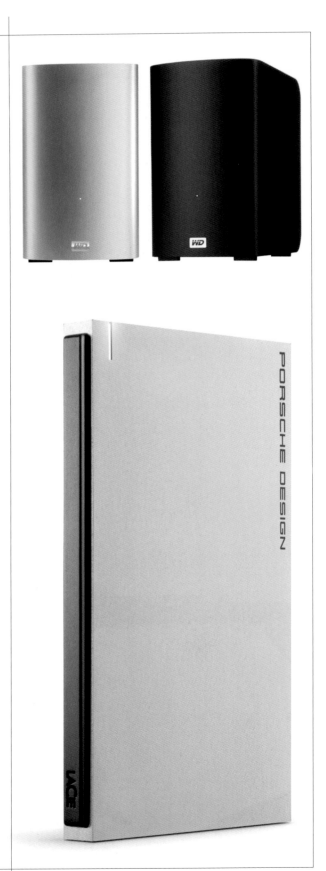

WD My Book
VelociRaptor Duo 2TB

You'd only pay £600 for 2TB of hard disk if you wanted the fastest money could buy. The twin 1TB drives here rotate at 10,000rpm, have 64MB of cache and use a 6Gbit/sec SATA-III interface, so the signs are good. Sure enough, at a steady 377.2MB/sec read and 348.9 to 365.2MB/sec write, yes, it's fast. And at least the Thunderbolt cable comes thrown in.

£599.99 from pcworld.co.uk
See wdc.com for details

LaCie Porsche Design
Slim SSD P'9223 120GB

With its uncompromising lines and sharp corners, this elegant external SSD is no bigger and barely heavier than some smartphones. It supports Time Machine and runs from your MacBook's USB 3 port without external power. LaCie quotes speeds of 'up to' 400MB/ sec. Reading, we hit this regularly; writing peaked at 200, averaging around a respectable 150MB/sec, far better than portable hard disks.

£135 from lacie.com/uk

Just Mobile
Xtand Pro and AluRack

Bringing together creative and engineering talent from Taiwan, Europe and Scandinavia, Just Mobile is a unique accessories manufacturer with a unique focus: Apple. These guys love Apple hardware and want nothing more than to create the add-ons it deserves. That means lots of aluminium, lots of attention to detail, and lots of design awards. It's well worth browsing around their website, but for now we'll draw your attention to one of their classic products and a relative newcomer. The Xtand Pro builds on the success of the Xtand, inspired by the first iPhone, and holds any MacBook firmly at one of two heights, bringing its screen up to your face while you type comfortably on your Apple Wireless Keyboard. The AluRack, on the other hand, is aimed at users who put their MacBook away at home and use an iMac. This precisely milled, neatly cushioned plate clamps to the cable cutout in the iMac's stand and holds the MacBook there, like an aluminium baby in a minimalist papoose. How have we not always done this?

£69 and **£49** from amazon.co.uk
See just-mobile.eu for details

Maxell
AirStash

iCloud is great as far as it goes, but there are still times when you need a simple, generic memory drive to get data from A to B – and iPhones and iPads lack a USB port to plug such things into. The AirStash equips an SD memory card (included) with a USB plug and its own wifi network, getting around all that. We even had iTunes movies playing from it on our iPad.

£91 from amazon.co.uk with 16GB
See maxellair.eu for details

Chapter 6
Maintenance

Watching for trouble

Your Mac shouldn't need a lot of maintenance, but if you keep an eye on how it's running, problems won't take you by surprise.

Perhaps the most important advice on keeping a Mac running smoothly is that you shouldn't have to do anything special to keep a Mac running smoothly. Unlike operating systems past (and a few present), OS X has only a very limited tendency to clog up and run slower and slower over time. There's no equivalent here of the monolithic Windows Registry, and although it's possible there might be a build-up over time of unneeded temporary files, settings files, files associated with apps you no longer use and so on, this almost invariably has absolutely no effect on the performance of your Mac, and takes up such a tiny proportion of your hard disk that it isn't worth worrying about. You're actually quite likely to do more harm than good if you insist on adding non-standard tools to 'housekeep' your Mac on a regular basis. It's really pretty good at cleaning up after itself.

On this note, defragmenting your hard disk, though often talked about, is not something you should need to do, since OS X constantly monitors fragmentation and has effective strategies to avoid it. That's why your Mac doesn't even come with a tool for it.

The only way it's likely to become an issue is if you let the amount of free space on your startup disk – the one with OS X installed on it – get too small. Generally, aim to keep 10-20% of a small hard disk or SSD free; that'll be overkill with, say, a 2TB drive, but 50-100GB is good. If you're down to single digits, in gigabytes, it's time to clear out some clutter.

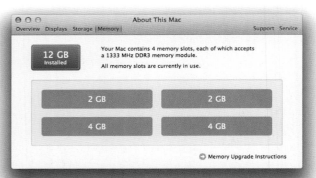

↑ **Don't overlook the extra tabs in About This Mac, accessed from the top of the Apple menu. This tab shows you what RAM is installed, if it's working, and how you could add more.**

↑ **The Storage tab shows your main hard disk, the startup disk (top), along with any others installed in or directly connected to your Mac. The icons indicate whether they're internal or external, and the graphs show what's on them.**

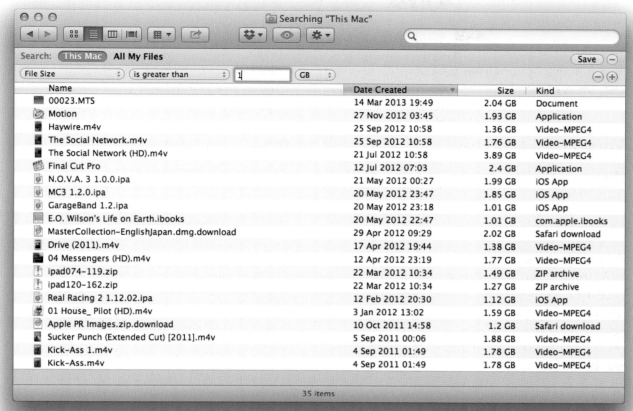

Name	Date Created	Size	Kind
00023.MTS	14 Mar 2013 19:49	2.04 GB	Document
Motion	27 Nov 2012 03:45	1.93 GB	Application
Haywire.m4v	25 Sep 2012 10:58	1.36 GB	Video-MPEG4
The Social Network.m4v	25 Sep 2012 10:58	1.76 GB	Video-MPEG4
The Social Network (HD).m4v	21 Jul 2012 10:58	3.89 GB	Video-MPEG4
Final Cut Pro	12 Jul 2012 07:03	2.4 GB	Application
N.O.V.A. 3 1.0.0.ipa	21 May 2012 00:27	1.99 GB	iOS App
MC3 1.2.0.ipa	20 May 2012 23:47	1.85 GB	iOS App
GarageBand 1.2.ipa	20 May 2012 23:18	1.01 GB	iOS App
E.O. Wilson's Life on Earth.ibooks	20 May 2012 22:47	1.01 GB	com.apple.ibooks
MasterCollection-EnglishJapan.dmg.download	29 Apr 2012 09:29	2.02 GB	Safari download
Drive (2011).m4v	17 Apr 2012 19:44	1.38 GB	Video-MPEG4
04 Messengers (HD).m4v	12 Apr 2012 23:19	1.77 GB	Video-MPEG4
ipad074–119.zip	22 Mar 2012 10:34	1.49 GB	ZIP archive
ipad120–162.zip	22 Mar 2012 10:34	1.27 GB	ZIP archive
Real Racing 2 1.12.02.ipa	12 Feb 2012 20:30	1.12 GB	iOS App
01 House_ Pilot (HD).m4v	3 Jan 2012 13:02	1.59 GB	Video-MPEG4
Apple PR Images.zip.download	10 Oct 2011 14:58	1.2 GB	Safari download
Sucker Punch (Extended Cut) [2011].m4v	5 Sep 2011 00:06	1.88 GB	Video-MPEG4
Kick-Ass 1.m4v	4 Sep 2011 01:49	1.78 GB	Video-MPEG4
Kick-Ass.m4v	4 Sep 2011 01:49	1.78 GB	Video-MPEG4

35 items

↑ It's easy to find big files to chuck out. Try sorting by Kind to help eliminate things like videos.

Checking disk usage

Every Finder window shows in its footer the amount of free space on the drive whose contents it's displaying. But if you have a number of drives attached it can be quite confusing to even figure out which one that is. For a much clearer indication of disk usage, go to the Apple menu and choose About This Mac, then click the Storage tab near the top left. You'll get a colour-coded chart of what's on which disk, with your startup disk at the top.

If at all possible, you should keep everything that's directly related to OS X, and all your apps, on the startup disk. But big folders of documents can move to external storage, as can your iTunes and iPhoto Libraries (as explained elsewhere in this book) and so on. Files you'll be accessing heavily, such as video footage you're editing, should be on as fast an interface as possible, so ideally on your startup disk; next best, another internal drive; failing that, the fastest drive on the fastest port you have (USB 3 or Thunderbolt).

Making room

Often some of the biggest files on your hard disk may be ones you don't need, such as disk images from app installations that you've completed. To find big files of any kind anywhere on your system, just open a Finder window (Cmd-N in the Finder), press Cmd-F to bring up the search criteria bar at the top, click the first option shown (such as Kind) and change this to File Size. If File Size isn't shown on the drop-down menu, pick Other and choose it from there. Now set the next option to 'is greater than'. Finally, set the units for the box at the right to GB, and type '1' in the box. You'll now see all the files bigger than a gigabyte. If you don't need one, delete it.

Although the move towards SSD is changing things (and bringing issues of its own), the hard disk is generally the most troublesome component in a Mac because it's one of the few mechanical parts, subject to wear and tear and unpredictable failure, and it's very heavily used. As we've mentioned, with today's all-multitasking operating systems you're likely to have far more apps open at once that will actually fit in RAM, so OS X will constantly be accessing the hard disk to swap data in and out of virtual memory. Over time, all kinds of minor, random corruption can occur, and your Mac begins to feel vaguely as if something isn't working smoothly.

Disk Utility

OS X comes with an app that tackles this kind of glitching, among other jobs. It's called Disk Utility, and like many other handy tools it lives in the Utilities folder inside Applications, although it's quicker to type its name into Spotlight than to go looking for it there. Open Disk Utility and you'll see your connected drives on the left and tasks that you might want to carry out on the right.

We'll ignore the Erase, RAID and Restore tabs for now, and so should you, unless you fully understand what you're doing. First Aid is the tab to be aware of. Select your startup disk on the left (the top one) and click the Verify Disk button on the right. As long as 'Show details' is ticked (you can tick it after the event if not), results should scroll rapidly up the box, and with a bit of luck Disk Utility will conclude 'The partition map appears to be OK.' If not, your next option is to click Repair Disk. This sounds dramatic, but is a relatively innocuous process that shouldn't do anything very exciting, but might well return your disk to normal.

However, you won't be able to repair the startup disk that contains the operating system that your Mac is currently running. If you need to do repairs on your startup disk, first restart the Mac from a different valid startup disk. The easiest way is to hold Cmd-R while you restart, to boot from the recovery partition. (On older Macs, insert the supplied system disc and boot from that instead, by holding C.) Once the Mac has started up in this limited OS X installation, run Disk Utility from the menus provided and do the repair.

Only if this reports that the disk can't be repaired should you start to worry, and consider getting hold of some more powerful (and less cheap) disk-fixing software, such as Alsoft DiskWarrior, or calling in some technical support.

Do bear in mind that a hard disk is very likely to die at some point during the working lifetime of a Mac, and replacing it, while often too fiddly to do yourself unless you're into that kind of thing, shouldn't be especially difficult or expensive. But this is why you must have a backup, so if you haven't set up Time Machine yet, see p42.

↓ Verifying your startup disk and repairing permissions is worth a try.

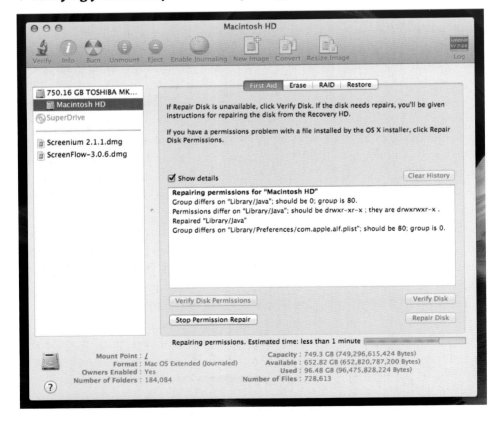

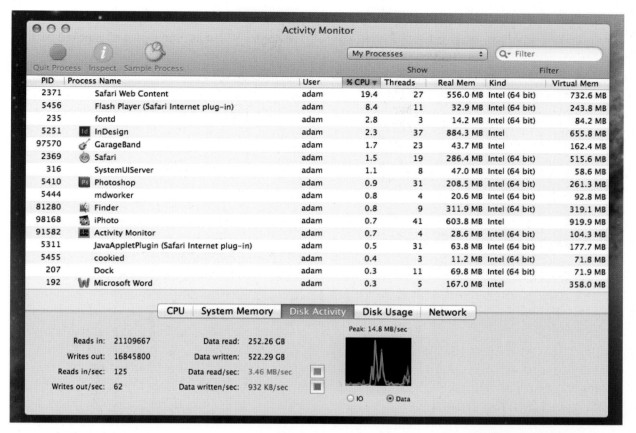

↑ A typical Activity Monitor report. Somewhere, a browser window with Flash content is hiding.

Notice that when the topmost hard disk icon is selected in the left column, the Verify Disk Permissions options are greyed out. Click the second disk icon down, though, and they come back. That's because this operation can only be done on that 'volume' within the drive. Although you can't see it, there's normally also a hidden recovery partition; if you have Windows installed under Boot Camp, there'll be a volume for that too, and so on.

Repairing permissions is a long-standing catch-all solution to Macs being glitchy, and just means making OS X check some settings on files that were created when you installed software. It's extremely unlikely to do any harm, so well worth doing now and again, or if something feels amiss.

When apps crash

Now and again, you'll notice a particular app failing to respond to your input, or perhaps refusing to come to the front when you try to Alt-Tab to it. It may just be having a long think (especially if it's Microsoft Excel), but chances are it's crashed. If you right-click its icon in the Dock, it may well report, in red, that the application is not responding. That's not conclusive, but suggestive. You can hold Alt to show a Force Quit option and pick that, or take a closer look at what's up.

The utility for this job is Activity Monitor. Open it (again, it lives in the Utilities folder inside Applications) and you'll see a display similar to the screenshot above. The drop-down menu at the top right can be used to choose whether to show all processes that are running, just those that are active, only 'My Processes' (those initiated by the currently logged-in user), or other options. One reason to pick My Processes is that you're unlikely to recognise processes that don't belong to you – there'll be a lot of obscure system stuff – so this helps narrow it down to, say, apps.

Apps that have crashed will appear in red here, and you can use the big shiny Quit Process button to force them to quit if you want to. But it's not always clear which app is the root cause of the crashing.

To help find out, click the column header 'CPU%' to sort the processes according to who's demanding most of the central processor chip's time. It may well be an app you didn't even know was supposed to be doing anything, a common example being the Flash plug-in for Safari, which will get itself in a state trying to render random ad graphics in web pages and end up bringing other apps down with it.

Try politely quitting (not force-quitting) any app that's using an inordinate amount of CPU time by right-clicking its Dock icon and choosing Quit. If you do need to force-quit apps, just give them a few seconds to clear up after themselves and you should invariably be able to open them again without any ill effects – except that, depending on their Versions compatibility or own-brand auto-save features, you may have lost any work you did in the app since your last save.

Using the Terminal

OS X may look very GUI, but it's based on the Unix operating system, which is very texty. The Terminal app, found in Utilities, literally opens a window onto this mysterious world. That's great if you're a Unix expert, but if you're not, it's an open invitation to execute commands that irretrievably mess up your system. Most users will only use Terminal once or twice, if at all, to fix a niggle or change a setting that isn't normally accessible. For example, if you don't like the way OS X hides your Library folder in the Finder's Go menu unless you hold the Alt key, you could open the Terminal and type:

```
chflags nohidden ~/Library
```

and press Return. But that would be up to you.

When the worst happens

If something's seriously amiss with your Mac, the usual symptoms are shutting down unexpectedly, perhaps with the terrifying Matrix-style rollerblind effect that Apple thoughtfully displays when a kernel panic occurs and the system halts to avoid damaging itself, or failing to start up after being powered off or asleep. Before trying to start up, make sure you're fully shut

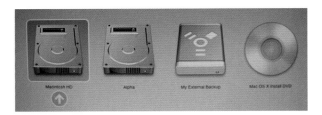

↑ **Startup Manager governs your startup disks.**

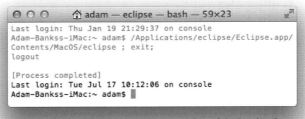

↑**Terminal: there's a reason why this isn't the default user interface – but it can be useful.**

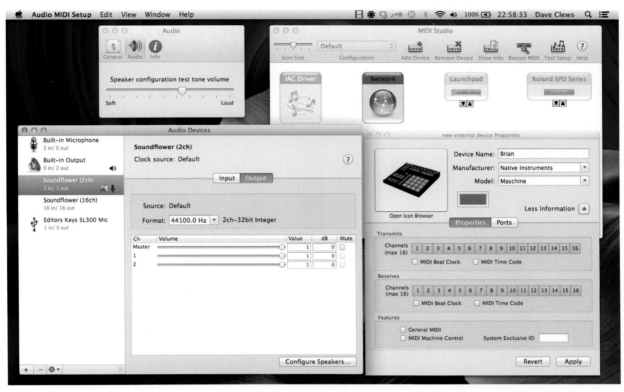

↑ **The Utilities folder contains some surprising gems, such as the Audio MIDI Setup tool, which lets you configure microphones, audio interfaces and other music peripherals to work with your Mac.**

down: turn off the power (hold the on/off button until you feel the machine go dead, or remove the mains plug if it's a desktop Mac), pause, then try starting up again. A flashing question mark is the Mac saying it can't find an operating system, which may mean there's a problem with your startup disk – but it may mean nothing, and go away after a couple more tries; or you may need to reselect the startup disk. Try restarting while holding Alt to bring up the Startup Manager, then tell the Mac where to look for OS X.

If nothing else is working, restart from the recovery partition by holding Cmd-R, or via Internet Recovery. This note from Apple explains: support.apple.com/kb/ht4718. You'll find plenty of advice at support.apple.com, but if you're stuck, work through the steps at apple.com/support/contact.

Apple only offers free tech support for the first 90 days after a product is sold, but you can make a free appointment at an Apple Store Genius Bar, if you can get to one with your Mac. If your Mac is quite new and has suddenly stopped working for no apparent reason, though, don't hesitate to phone Apple and ask for assistance under warranty or, in the UK, under the Sale of Goods Act – it's your right to have faulty goods promptly replaced, or repaired if they're a little older.

CLEAN-UP CREW

If you feel the urge to spring-clean your system, there are several apps for the job. Note that Trojans, adware and nagware sometimes present themselves as cleanup utilities, so look for reviews of anything you're thinking of installing. Among the utilities often recommended are the nearly-free Disk Doctor from MacGems and the more comprehensive (but pricier) CleanMyMac from Macpaw. For the more technically inclined, Cocktail, from Maintain, tackles a different selection of issues and is popular with geekier users.

Gesture gallery

Two-finger scrolling Drag up or down with two fingers within an app window to scroll its contents.

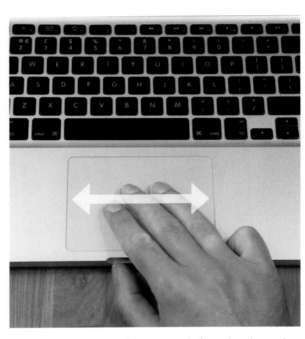

Three-finger switching Drag left and right with three fingers to switch between full-screen apps.

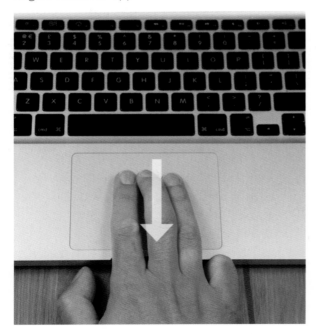

Mission Control Drag down with three fingers to enter Mission Control and view your desktops.

Double-tap zoom Similar to Safari on the iPhone, double-tap with two fingers to zoom on a website.

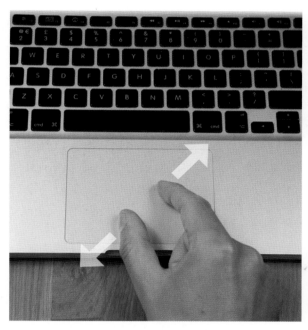

Unpinch to stretch Enlarge an image or website by unpinching two fingers on top of it.

Back off by pinching Pinch back in again to zoom out of a web page or application window.

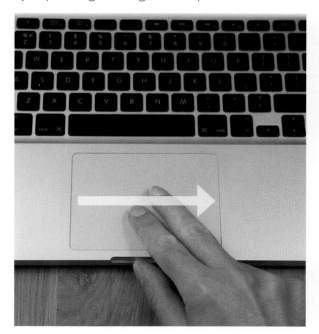

Swipe to turn pages Slide two fingers sideways across the trackpad to leaf through documents.

Grip to launch Put all five fingers on the trackpad and close them up to open Launchpad.

Glossary

AirPlay Apple's proprietary system for streaming audio or video from one device to another

Drag Click the primary mouse button while the pointer is over an item, then hold while moving the mouse to take the item to a different location

GB Gigabyte, 1,024 or 1,000 megabytes

GUI Graphical user interface – a user interface based on pictorial representations rather than, for example, text commands

Hard disk Mechanical device that reads data from and writes data to a spinning magnetic platter

iCloud Online service operated by Apple
User interface Means by which a person controls software, usually comprising a screen display

iOS Apple's mobile operating system, used by the iPhone, iPad and iPod touch

Macintosh Personal computer brand invented by Apple and first released in 1984

MB Megabyte, 1,024 kilobytes

MB/sec Megabytes per second, typically measuring an amount of data actually transferred

Mbit/sec Megabits per second (also 'Mbps'), typically citing a theoretical transfer speed

OS Operating system – the software a computer needs before it can manage files and run apps

Pointer On-screen indicator moved by a mouse or trackpad (also 'cursor')

RAM Random access memory, the fast but non-permanent memory used to run programs

Right-click Click with a secondary button on a mouse or trackpad, or an equivalent gesture

SSD Solid state drive, a term for flash memory packaged to serve the purpose of a hard disk

TB Terabyte, 1,024 or 1,000 gigabytes

Thunderbolt Peripheral interface backed by Apple, offering very fast connection speeds

Trackpad Sensor plate that translates touch into signals governing actions on screen

iTunes Apple's digital entertainment service and associated software

Wi-Fi Set of standards constituting today's interoperable wireless networks (also 'wifi')

THE **INDEPENDENT** GUIDE TO THE APPLE
MacBook

Editor in Chief and Creative Director
Adam Banks
for Vast Landscape Ltd

Writer
Nik Rawlinson

Digital Production Manager
Nicky Baker

Advertising
MagBook Advertising Director Katie Wood
Senior MagBook Executive Emma D'Arcy

Management
MagBook Publisher Dharmesh Mistry
Operations Director Robin Ryan
MD of Advertising Julian Lloyd-Evans
Newstrade Director David Barker
MD of Enterprise Martin Belson
Chief Operating Officer Brett Reynolds
Group Finance Director Ian Leggett
Chief Executive James Tye
Chairman Felix Dennis

The MagBook brand is a trademark of Dennis Publishing Ltd, 30 Cleveland St, London W1T 4JD. Company registered in England. All material © Dennis Publishing Ltd, licensed by Felden 2013, and may not be reproduced in whole or part without the consent of the publishers.

The Independent Guide to the Apple MacBook ISBN 1–78106–229–3

Licensing and Syndication
To license this product, please contact Carlotta Serantoni on +44 (0) 20 7907 6550 or email carlotta_serantoni@dennis.co.uk.
To syndicate content from this product, please contact Anj Dosaj Halai on +44(0) 20 7907 6132 or email anj_dosaj-halai@dennis.co.uk

Liability
While every care was taken during the production of this MagBook, the publishers cannot be held responsible for the accuracy of the information or any consequence arising from it. Dennis Publishing takes no responsibility for the companies advertising in this MagBook.

The paper used within this MagBook is produced from sustainable fibre, manufactured by mills with a valid chain of custody. Printed by Polestar Bicester.

MacUser